Michael George Mulhall

**Rio Grande do Sul and its German Colonies**

Michael George Mulhall

**Rio Grande do Sul and its German Colonies**

ISBN/EAN: 9783337152529

Printed in Europe, USA, Canada, Australia, Japan

Cover: Foto ©ninafisch / pixelio.de

More available books at **www.hansebooks.com**

# RIO GRANDE DO SUL

AND

ITS GERMAN COLONIES.

BY

MICHAEL G. MULHALL.

LONDON:
LONGMANS, GREEN, AND CO.
1873.

*All rights reserved.*

# PREFACE.

LAST SUMMER I made an excursion to Rio Grande, where I was astonished to find so many thriving German colonies, of which little is known in the River Plate or in Europe. The only works I could find referring to so interesting a part of the Brazilian Empire were a pamphlet written in German and reproduced in French at Paris some twenty years ago, and a 'Cuadro Estadistico' by the engineer Camargo, published at Port Alegre in 1868. My impressions and notes of travel through the colonies were too voluminous for reproduction in the columns of a daily paper, and for that reason I publish them in the present form, including some letters which have already appeared in the Buenos Ayres 'Standard.' To my readers I will only say, that for a pleasure-trip during vacation I can strongly recommend Port Alegre, its beautiful scenery and kindly people; so little known to the outer world, although only twenty days from London by steamer, and three from the River Plate. Passengers from England would have to change at Rio Janeiro from the ocean-steamer to Lamport and Holt's line, and again at Rio Grande to Proudfoot's lake-steamer 'Guayiba.' Those from the River Plate can take Lamport and Holt's fortnightly steamer from Monte Video, the passage to Rio Grande averaging thirty hours. The artist or sportsman will find plenty of occupation ascending the Jacuhy, Sinos, Caby, and other fine rivers which have their confluence at Port Alegre. Should this little book be of any utility, my recollections of a vacation spent among the German colonies will be all the more pleasurable.

M. G. MULHALL.

BUENOS AYRES: *June* 10, 1872.

| | | |
|---|---|---|
| Preface | | v |
| Introduction | | 1 |

CHAPTER
| | | |
|---|---|---|
| I. | Province of Rio Grande | 12 |
| II. | City of Rio Grande | 39 |
| III. | Rio Grande to Port Alegre | 49 |
| IV. | Port Alegre | 55 |
| V. | The Suburbs of Port Alegre | 59 |
| VI. | English Enterprises in Port Alegre | 65 |
| VII. | The New Hamburg Railway | 72 |
| VIII. | The Coalfields of San Jeronimo | 78 |
| IX. | Excursion to San Leopoldo | 85 |
| X. | Inauguration of the San Leopoldo Railway | 94 |
| XI. | A Ride through the Colonies | 105 |
| XII. | From the Waterfall to the Devil's Glen | 114 |
| XIII. | German Colonies—History and Progress | 123 |
| XIV. | Arrial and Pelotas | 153 |
| XV. | Yaguaron and Lake Mini | 173 |
| VI. | German Colonies in Santa Catharina | 187 |

# RIO GRANDE DO SUL.

### INTRODUCTION.

The Empire of Brazil has made great strides in the last few years, not only in all branches of material progress, but also in the enlightened policy which has found such strenuous supporters in Dom Pedro Segundo and his minister, Viscount Paranhos do Rio Branco. The Emancipation law of 1871 is now being followed up by an extensive programme of English and German immigration, and a great effort to diffuse instruction among the lower orders of the people.

It may not be out of place to give the reader an outline of this immense and fertile region, which occupies the half of South America, and contains twenty provinces, each of which is larger than an empire or kingdom in Europe. The largest, Matto Grosso, is ten times the size of

England; the smallest, Espirito Santo, is almost as big as Belgium and Holland put together. The coast-line on the Atlantic is nearly 4,000 miles long. The water-courses are unrivalled; steamboats can navigate the Amazon and tributaries a length of 22,000 miles, and for the last twenty years a regular line of steamers has plied between Para and Tabatinga, on the Amazon proper, a distance of 1,800 miles. Numerous mountain chains are met with, the highest being Serra Itatiaia, over 10,000 feet in elevation. Forests cover a great portion of the interior, and the mineral wealth, especially in gold and diamonds, is very remarkable. The population is put down at 11,000,000, including 1,400,000 slaves, and 500,000 untamed Indians. By the new Emancipation law, which provides for gradual abolition, there will be no slavery by the close of this century. The institutions of the country are extremely liberal, the Government being a kind of Federal Republic, with an Emperor instead of a President. The established religion is the Roman Catholic, but the utmost liberty and equality may be said to exist in this and all other matters affecting foreigners, who find also the greatest protection for life and property. The army, in time of peace, counts 25,000 men; the navy, consisting chiefly of iron-clads and gunboats, is manned by 5,546 sailors.

The growth of the national revenues is prodigious: at the accession of the present Emperor, in 1832, they amounted to 11,000,000 mr. (say 1,100,000*l*.); in 1864 they had risen to 60,000,000, and in 1871 to 94,000,000, or 9,500,000*l*. sterling, the budget for this last year (at 10 milreis per £) standing thus:—

| Revenue | |
|---|---|
| Import duties | £5,250,000 |
| Export „ | 1,896,000 |
| Licenses | 1,080,000 |
| Railways | 400,000 |
| Property tax | 350,000 |
| Miscellaneous | 424,000 |
| | £9,400,000 |

| Expenditure | |
|---|---|
| Imperial household | £140,000 |
| Senators and deputies | 70,000 |
| Army and navy | 2,150,000 |
| Justice | 340,000 |
| Foreign affairs | 80,000 |
| Interior | 177,000 |
| Railways and steamers | 700,000 |
| Post and telegraph | 130,000 |
| Immigration | 85,000 |
| Public institutes | 300,000 |
| Worship | 125,000 |
| Finance | 1,600,000 |
| Interest on debt | 2,332,000 |
| Surplus | 1,171,000 |
| | £9,400,000 |

The Emperor's salary is 40,000*l*. per annum, that of the Empress 4,800*l*. The budget for 1872 puts down 93,000,000 mr. for income, and 86,000,000 mr.

for expenditure, leaving a surplus of 7,000,000 mr., or 700,000*l.* sterling.

The national debt amounts to 650,000,000 mr., or 65,000,000*l.* sterling, of which one-half has been caused by the Paraguayan war, its growth being as follows:—

| 1865 | . . | £30,800,000 | 1869 | . . | £59,000,000 |
| 1866 | . . | 38,100,000 | 1870 | . . | 64,400,000 |
| 1867 | . . | 50,500,000 | 1871 | . . | 64,900,000 |
| 1868 | . . | 58,000,000 | | | |

The national debt is made up thus:—

| | Millions sterling |
|---|---|
| Foreign loans . . . . . . . | 16 |
| Government stock or home debt . . . | 30 |
| Paper money . . . . . . . | 15 |
| Orphan fund, &c. . . . . . . | 2½ |
| War bills unpaid . . . . . . | 1½ |
| | 65 millions |

Henceforward this debt will go steadily downwards, as the budget each year shows a surplus. Meantime a debt of 65,000,000*l.* sterling is only trifling when compared with the revenue or population of the empire, being only seven years' income, or equal to 6*l.* per head of the population.

Brazil has no fewer than seven loans in London, the balances due on each standing thus:—

| | |
|---|---|
| 1852 | £685,800 |
| 1858 | 861,500 |
| 1859 | 335,200 |
| 1860 | 944,100 |
| 1863 | 3,035,700 |
| 1865 | 6,573,600 |
| 1871 | 3,459,600 |
| | £15,895,500 |

It will be seen that two-thirds of the money borrowed in England went to the expenses of the war, the total cost of which is officially stated at 39,000,000*l*. sterling, so that about three-fourths of this amount was raised in the country by home loans, paper money, or taxation. It is right to note here that besides 151,000,000 mr. in Government notes the bank of Brazil has an issue of 36,500,000, and other banks 2,000,000 in paper money, making the total of paper currency 189,500,000 mr., or 19,000,000*l*. sterling.

So far from the Paraguayan War causing the trade or products of Brazil to fall off, the increase in that period was wonderful, as will be seen in the three great staples which make up the exports of the empire, comparing 1870 with 1860, thus:—

| | 1870 | 1860 |
|---|---|---|
| Coffee | 186,841 tons | 151,794 tons |
| Sugar | 129,243 „ | 115,210 „ |
| Cotton | 41,188 „ | 14,295 „ |

This shows that, in spite of the war, the products have increased enormously, viz.—twenty-four per cent. in coffee, twelve per cent. in sugar, and nearly two hundred per cent. in cotton. Of this last staple San Paulo alone yielded last year 30,000 tons.

If we compare the returns of the year (1864) previous to the breaking out of the war with the subsequent ones, the result is equally satisfactory. The tables are in arrobes of thirty-five lbs. each.

| Year | Cotton | Sugar | Coffee | India-rubber |
|------|--------|-------|--------|--------------|
| 1864 | 1,350,465 | 8,016,127 | 8,183,311 | 23,235 |
| 1865 | 1,726,015 | 7,483,107 | 10,806,336 | 232,417 |
| 1866 | 2,899,004 | 9,158,065 | 9,940,566 | 230,900 |
| 1867 | 2,689,206 | 8,167,685 | 13,048,464 | 325,636 |
| 1868 | 3,386,692 | 8,719,023 | 14,546,770 | 343,422 |

Thus we see that in four years the produce of the country almost doubled, the increase under the various headings being—in cotton one hundred and fifty per cent., sugar nine per cent., coffee eighty per cent., India-rubber forty-four per cent. If we take the four items in one bulk we find Brazil exported in 1864 about 300,000 tons of produce, and in 1868 over 450,000 tons. The value of these four items in 1864 was 54,000,000 hard dollars, and in 1868 was 74,000,000.

The imports and exports of the various provinces in 1869 stood thus :—

|  | Imports | Exports |
|---|---|---|
|  | £ sterling | £ sterling |
| Rio Janeyro | 9,000,000 | 9,000,000 |
| Pernambuco | 2,560,000 | 2,310,000 |
| Bahia | 2,350,000 | 2,160,000 |
| Pará | 820,000 | 1,080,000 |
| Rio Grande do Sul | 770,000 | 856,000 |
| Maranhao | 520,000 | 607,800 |
| Ceará | 325,600 | 488,800 |
| San Paolo | 230,000 | 1,780,000 |
| Eight other provinces | 84,400 | 1,986,000 |
|  | £16,660,000 | £20,268,600 |

Brazil takes half her imports from England, one-fourth from France, and the rest from the River Plate, United States and Portugal. She exports half her produce to England, one-eighth to France, one-eighth to North America, and the rest to other countries. Her coasting trade, not included above, stands for about 5,000,000*l.* sterling, being carried on by 3,200 vessels, averaging 200 tons each, and manned by 45,000 sailors; besides 120 coasting steamers.

There are eighteen banks in Brazil, which may be briefly set down thus :—

|  | Capital | Observations |
|---|---|---|
| Bank of Brazil | £3,300,000 | Emission 4,000,000*l.* |
| London and Brazilian | 1,500,000 | Branches at Bahia, Santos, &c. |
| English Bank | 1,000,000 | Branches like above |
| Rural Bank | 800,000 | Deposits 2,000,000*l.* |
| Commercial Bank | 1,200,000 | One-sixth paid up |
| Campos Bank | 100,000 | Dividend 11 per cent. |
| Bahia Bank | 800,000 | Emission 180,000*l.* |
| Bahia Reserve | 400,000 | Half paid up |
| Bahia Mortgage | 120,000 | Dividend 7 per cent. |
| Bahia Savings | 300,000 | Dividend 7 per cent. |
| Bahia Commercial | 560,000 | Dividend $7\frac{3}{4}$ per cent. |
| Bahia Economy | 62,000 | Dividend $7\frac{1}{2}$ per cent. |
| Pernambuco Bank |  | In liquidation |
| Alâgoas Bank | 30,000 | Dividend 12 per cent. |
| Maranhao Bank | 100,000 | Dividend $13\frac{1}{2}$ per cent. |
| Maranhao Commercial | 200,000 | Half paid |
| Parà Commercial | 80,000 | Deposits 200,000*l.* |
| Rio Grande do Sul | 100,000 | Dividend 11 per cent. |

The prosperous condition of Brazilian finances and trade, causes the national securities to be in great request as well in England as in Brazil. The Brazilian bonds on the London Stock Exchange are usually above par, and the Home Debt six per cents. at Rio Janeyro may be quoted at par, while the 'gold' bonds' are at ten per cent. premium; the last amount to about 3,000,000*l.* sterling, with coupons payable in specie instead of paper money, which causes them to be a favourite investment with people abroad, as it gives them five and a-half per cent for their money. Besides the local six per cents., there are also a series of four and five per cents., the entire home debt being, as above stated, about 30,000,000*l.* sterling.

There are four principal lines of railway open to traffic, besides numerous branches or lines of less importance, and about 1,800 miles of telegraph actually working.

The Pedro Segundo Railway was begun in 1857, and the first section, 30 miles, opened in the following year to Queimados. At present more than 150 miles are open to traffic, and the line is being prolonged to the Tocantins river. The Government has expended over 3,000,000*l.* sterling on this line: the gross receipts average ten per cent. and the net proceeds more than six per cent. on the cost of construction.

The San Paulo line has already cost over 2,500,000*l.* sterling, and belongs not to the State but to an English Joint Stock Company, the Imperial Government possessing shares to the value of 100,000*l.* The net proceeds average over five per cent., and when the new branches are open the traffic will be much increased. The working expenses are only one-third of the gross receipts.

The Bahia line was opened in 1860, and its

traffic was so small that for nearly ten years the annual receipts did not cover working expenses; the deficit had to be made good out of the seven per cent. guarantee of the Imperial Government. At the close of 1868 the aggregate deficit for eight years amounted to 120,000*l*. Since then the affairs of the line have been every year improving. The Government shares represent 20,000*l*.

The Pernambuco line cost 1,825,000*l*., being fifty per cent. over the original estimates upon which the Government guarantee was given, on a length of 80 miles. The Imperial Government holds 700,000*l*. worth of shares. The working expenses are two-thirds of the gross receipts, and the shareholders' dividend chiefly depends on the Government guarantee.

There are no fewer than fifteen lesser railways or branches being constructed, besides numerous roads, canals, bridges, docks, and other public works of the most useful description. At the same time a submarine cable to unite Brazil with Europe is being contracted for by Baron Manà, who engages to have it complete before the end of 1874. Another great enterprise is the diversion of Bolivian trade from the Pacific to the Amazon by means of Colonel Church's Mamorè and Madera

Railway, which will connect the settled parts of Bolivia with the head-waters of the chief affluents of the Amazon.

But far surpassing all other schemes in magnitude is that of importing thousands of Germans and Englishmen to colonise the splendid provinces of Rio Grande, San Paulo, Santa Catalina, &c. Messrs. Crawfurd, Kitts, and Hodgskin have arrived in Rio Janeyro to arrange for sending out 150,000 English emigrants in batches up to 10,000 yearly. At the same time contracts have been concluded for 40,000 Germans to San Paulo, 60,000 to Rio Grande, and other smaller numbers for elsewhere; showing that colonisation is now the great aim of the Brazilian Government.

# I.

## PROVINCE OF RIO GRANDE.

At the southern extremity of the vast empire of Brazil we find the rich and favoured province of Rio Grande do Sul, otherwise called San Pedro, which, although one of the smallest provinces of Brazil, is yet three times the size of England, having an area of 8,925 square leagues (of 16 square miles each), or 142,800 square miles English. Its situation between the twenty-ninth and thirty-fourth parallels of south latitude, gives it a finer and more temperate climate than any other part of the empire.

It is bounded on the north by the provinces of St. Catherine's and Parana, on the south by the republic of Banda Oriental, on the east by the Atlantic Ocean, and on the west by the Upper Uruguay, which separates it from the Argentine Misiones and Corrientes. By the treaty of 1852, the frontier with the Oriental Republic was defined as the mouth of the Chuy on the Atlantic, and the mouth of the Quareim on the Uruguay. The frontier line had been a constant bone of contention in the time of Spaniards and Portuguese, and no fewer than three special commissions, in 1759, 1789, and 1790, were sent to mark the limits on the part of the two Crowns, and at last agreed to the mouth of the Pepiry-Guassù, which is now the point of demarcation between the Brazilian and Argentine territories.

Its greatest measurement from east to west is 500 miles, and from north to south 400 miles. A range of hills, called the Coxilha Grande, traverses the country from north to south, forming two watersheds, the eastern with an area of 4,325, the western 4,600 square leagues. At the same time an equally remarkable bisection of the country is made by the Serra Geral, running east and west, all the northern half being high and mountainous, the southern low but undulating. The Serra Geral is sometimes called Serra do Mir, and all the other ranges, Serra Herval, Tapes, Pinhal, San Javier, are so many ramifications.

The country is magnificently wooded and watered, and the mountain ranges add to its picturesque appearance, although no higher than the hills of Derbyshire. The highest point of the Sierra Geral is Passo Santa Victoria, 3,200 feet over the sea-level.

The principal rivers are—the Jacuhy, Gravatahy, Sinos, Cahy, Guayiba, Camaquan, San Gonzalo, Yaguaron, Quarahim, Pepiry-Guassù, Ibicuhy, Upper Uruguay, and tributaries.

The Jacuhy is the most considerable of the four affluents which form the splendid estuary of Guayiba. It rises near Cruz Alta in the Serra Geral, waters the towns of Cachoeira, Rio Pardo, Santo Amaro, Triumfo and San Jeronimo, and debouches in front of Port Alegre : it has often a width of 700 feet, and the current sometimes runs up to five miles an hour. It is navigable for steamers to Rio Pardo (120 miles), and in times of high water to Cachoeira, 80 miles higher up. Among its tributaries are—Rio Pardo, which bathes the Santa Cruz colony; Taquary, the most rapid water-course in the province; and Arroyo dos Ratos, famous for its coal-fields.

The Gravatahy rises in the Coxilha das Lombas, and is only navigable about 20 miles, but in high water, boats go up to Aldea dos Anjos, 30 miles from the embouchure at Port Alegre.

## PROVINCE OF RIO GRANDE. 15

The Rio dos Sinos is 120 miles long, from its head-waters at Pedras Blancas to its mouth, and takes its name from its sinuous course. It is the most important river in the province as an industrial highroad, being the great outlet for the products of San Leopoldo and many of the other colonies. It is navigated by steamers daily, at all seasons, from Port Alegre to San Leopoldo, 56 miles, and, unless at low water, as far as Mundo Novo, 60 miles higher.

The Cahy has its head-waters at Cima da Serra, and runs 120 miles, being navigable for half that distance, from Port Alegre to Port Guimaraes; one of its tributaries, the Cadea, has a waterfall of 730 feet perpendicular near the Herval colonies, and is navigable some 20 miles up to Hortenseschneitz. The Marata, which washes the Paricy and other colonies, is also navigable for lumberboats. Several other tributaries water numerous German colonies in their course.

The majestic Guayiba, formed of the above four rivers, forms a beautiful estuary or inland sea, in the midst of which rises the picturesque promontory on which stands Port Alegre, the capital of Rio Grande. After a course of 35 miles it debouches into Lake Patos, where its mouth is guarded by the peaks of Stapoa and Morro da Formiga.

The Camaquan rises in Santa Tecla hills near Bagè, and has a rapid course to Lake Patos, debouching by three mouths.

The San Gonzalo is a canal 50 miles long, connecting the two great lakes, Mirim and Patos, and watering the important city of Pelotas. It is the medium of an active trade with Rio Grande and the outer world, and the dredging of the bar, which is now going on, will facilitate its navigation to vessels of large burthen. The Arroyo Pelotas is a tributary navigable for 20 miles, and the Piratinin, which debouches 35 miles above the city of Pelotas, is remarkable for a grand stone bridge recently erected by Government.

The Yaguaron rises in the Serra Asseguà, near Bagè, and falls into Lake Mirim, after serving for frontier limit between Brazil and the Republic of Uruguay. Twenty miles from its mouth is the important town of Yaguaron.

The Quarahim, or Cuareim, which serves as the frontier limit with Banda Oriental, is an affluent of the Upper Uruguay.

The Pepiry-Guassù is the limit between Brazil and the Misiones of Corrientes, and falls into the

Uruguay about four miles above the waterfall known as Salto Grande.

The Ibicuy, which has no fewer than thirty-five tributaries, debouches into the Uruguay a little above the town of Uruguayana.

The Uruguay in its entire length has a course of 1,000 miles, from the Serra do Mar, in the province of Sta Catarina, to its confluence with the Paraná in forming the estuary of La Plata. It flows for 600 miles through Brazilian territory until reaching the mouth of the Cuareim: this portion may be termed the Upper Uruguay, inaccessible to vessels unless in great floods, there being numerous rapids and waterfalls. At Cachoeira do Mulato three barriers of rocks are met with, each about 30 feet high; at Xapecò the rapids extend for two miles, and are generally impassable; at Fortaleza a wall of rock runs across the river, and in flood-time the central part looks exactly like a fortress. But the finest of all is the Salto Grande, which is 35 feet in height and 2,500 yards long, running not across the river but longitudinally, leaving a channel of 45 yards on the left bank: in other words, a river of 700 yards in width is here compressed into this narrow channel for half a league. A scientific expedition sent hither in 1863 discovered cylindrical cavities in the rocks similar to those mentioned by Lyell as found near Norwich in 1839, and known in France as '*puits naturels*.' From Salto Grande, descending the Uruguay, sundry small cataracts are met with before reaching the mouth of the Cuareim. In flood-seasons, steamers of light draught ascend from the River Plate and Lower Uruguay to the city of Uruguayana, near the mouth of the Ibicuy. That part of Misiones traversed by the Uruguay in its earlier course is mountainous and thickly wooded: at times, basaltic rocks rise on either side of the river, which has an average width of from 300 to 500 yards, and runs seven miles an hour. The first signs of habitation are met with at Passo Fundo, where there are sugar and yerba factories, and here also the muleteers of San Paulo cross the Uruguay, which is about 35 feet deep. Then a stretch of 400 miles, through varied scenery, is wholly uninhabited till reaching the town of San Borja, opposite to which is the old missionary village of St°. Fomé, in Corrientes. Lower down are the town of Itaquy and city of Uruguayana.

Besides its great river system, Rio Grande possesses two immense lakes which are also convenient high-roads for commerce. Lake Mirim, called by the Indian and Spanish settlers Mini, is a vast inland sea 115 miles long by 15 wide, fed by the rivers Yaguaron, Taquary, and twenty lesser streams, one-half of which have their rise in the Banda Oriental, between which country and Brazil this lake serves as frontier, but its waters are declared Brazilian territory by the treaty with Monte Video. Lake Patos, like the former, is at the same level as the ocean, from which it is only separated by a strip of low sandy territory, and is larger than Mirim, its greatest length being 140 miles, and its greatest width 40. The two lakes communicate by the San Gonzalo river, and the waters of both form the estuary of Rio Grande, which runs 50 miles to the sea, washing the seaport city of the same name and debouching into the Atlantic over a dangerous bar. The entire coast-line of the province is low and sandy, beaten by the Atlantic, and without any accessible port or entrance save the dangerous one at the bar.

The geological formation of the country plainly shows that the coast-line of the Atlantic formerly followed the Serra do Mar, Itapoa, and the Tapes and Herval ranges; the low-lying sandy formation about Lake Mirim and Rio Grande is more recent. The city of Rio Grande is only 28 inches over sea-level. Geologists might be able to fix the period at which all this portion of the country was covered by the Atlantic, from the fact that oyster-shells have been found at Itapoa Hill, 14 feet above sea-level. Along the sea-shore there is a line of dunes, or sand-hills, which shift their position under the action of the wind. Mr. Frederick Sellow reports the hill-ranges of Herval and Tapes to be of primitive formation, and all the country north and west of basaltic rock, besides transition porphyry in many places, adding that this is the only part of Brazil where basalt and porphyry are found, and that geologists for a long time denied the existence of such formations east of the Andes. Another geologist, named Plant, says the mineral wealth of this province holds out promise of a glorious future. Iron and coal are found in many places; the western hill-ranges are rich in metals; gold abounds in the Cuñapiru district near Banda Oriental. At the same time the forests which cover almost the entire country, and the navigable rivers in all directions, offer every incentive to industry, and present (says Mr. Plant) such a combination of favourable circumstances as would indicate that

Providence had destined Rio Grande to play a conspicuous part in the world's progress. The minerals are as yet unexplored for the most part, but two companies have just been formed in London for the working of the coal-fields of Candiota and Arroyo dos Ratos, which were first discovered in 1809, and have at various times been worked at intervals. Near the Uruguay and its affluents are found quantities of agate, cornelian, rock-crystal, opals, &c., which are exported to Europe. Councillor Correa Camara gives a list of minerals found at various places, which may be summarised thus:—

Gold at Piratiny, Encrusilhada, and San Gabriel.

Silver, iron, and granite at Piratiny; also nitrate of potash and Glauber salts.

Copper in the Misiones, bordering on Upper Uruguay, and at Caçapava.

Marble and malachite at Caçapava, Bagè, and Rio Pardo.

· Iron at Encrusilhada, Caçapava, and Cachoeira.

Coal at Candiota, Arroyo Ratos, Curral Alto, and Cachoeira.

There is little or no trace of volcanic agency in any part of the province, but the inhabitants of

Port Alegre say there was a shock of earthquake in that city in 1811; and a water-spout, accompanied by a loud report like cannon, occurred at the mouth of the Jacuhy in 1822.

In the vegetable kingdom this province is extraordinarily rich. The late distinguished Austrian botanist, Martins, classified the chief products in his work on the Flora of Brazil. The woods which cover the Serra Geral and its branches, and which are so luxuriant in the valleys of the Uruguay, Jacuhy, Taquary, and other rivers, abound in excellent timber for building, such as cabriuva, angico, cedar, guajuvira, timbanba, grapia-punha, açouta-cavallo, iron-wood, black and brown canella, rose-wood or jacarandà, ipè or tecoma speciosa, peroba, cambosin, pinho, tajuba, cangerana, capororoca, sobragy, louro, caroba, pine, vinhatico, &c. The largest trees belong to the genus known among botanists as dycotyledons, embracing the various families of urtigacea, euphorbiacea, laurinea, leguminosa, myrtacea, &c. In the forests are also met with, in great profusion, ferns, orchids, bromelia, convulenlacea, aroidea, bignonia, cipò, paniflora, lichen, liliacea, and an infinity of creeping plants. Among the brushwood are shrubs of some estimation, such as araucaria braziliana, cocus flexuosa, schinus terebinthifolius, balsam, agave, bromelia bracteala, malvacea, apocynea, &c. The medicinal plants are numberless, the principal being—quinine, ipecacuanha, rhubarb, sarsaparilla, cipò mucunà, paraguay tea, poaia, &c. The fruits of the tropics as well as of cold climates thrive admirably, such as the orange, lime, banana, apple, pear, fig, Damascus cherry, plum, apricot, grape, lemon, amygdalus pessica, jaboticadeira, pitangeira, goyabeira, ananazeiro, marmello, jambo, arazà, ameixa, amora, melon, gabirova, cidra, melancia, &c. The cereals and crops comprise—maize, mandioca, beans, rice, tobacco, sugar, cotton, arrowroot, indigo, wheat, barley, flax, potatoes, linseed, oats, oil-plant, &c. The soil is so rich as to be inexhaustible, and needs no manure. Fully one-half the province is still covered with virgin forest, and in the water-shed of the Uruguay there is a tract of 40 miles in width by 400 in length, where the timber is gigantic.

The climate is what an Englishman would consider rather warm, but mild and agreeable compared to that of India, or even to the temperature of the northern parts of Brazil. It is not unlike that of Sicily or Algiers, but probably not so dry, and proves exceedingly healthy not only to native Brazilians but to the thousands of German colonists.

Summer commences with January, autumn with April, winter with July, and spring with October; but the seasons are not so clearly defined as in Europe, and may be properly divided into the cold and warm. In the higher lands the cold season is sometimes accompanied with snow; and when the Minuano, or icy wind from the Andes, blows you will often see a thin coating of ice on the lakes, which, however, melts before the noon-day sun. The month of May is remarkable for what is termed Veranico de Mayo, which something resembles the Indian summer of North America. The coldest months usually are June and July. In summer the average temperature of the hottest months, January and February, is 72° at 6 in the morning, 90° at noon, and 81° at 6 P.M., but it sometimes touches 95° at noon. In winter it ranges from 50° at sunrise to 65° at noon, and 60° at sunset. The days vary little in length all the year round, as is a necessary consequence of the latitude. The greatest variations of temperature occur usually at 2 in the afternoon and the same hour in the morning. Fogs are very common in May and August, lasting till about 11 A.M., and often followed by heavy rain, with thunder. After the west wind, or Minuano, has

## PROVINCE OF RIO GRANDE. 25

blown the atmosphere clears up, and frost ensues, the ice in such elevated points as Cima da Serra lasting for three or four days. The north-east wind begins at the close of winter, usually in October, and lasts till January or even March. It clears the atmosphere of the miasmas which arise from the overflow of lakes and rivers in the winter, and often brings rain and thunder for a couple of days. The north and nor'west winds bring a rise of temperature, with rain and thunder. The south and east winds are unhealthy and variable, the former sometimes blowing for two or three days consecutively in winter. The west wind is known to blow ten or fifteen days without intermission. The Atlantic sea-board is lashed with frequent storms. Rainy weather is generally accompanied with thunder, at all seasons; hail-storms are rarely seen.

The naturalist or sportsman would find abundant occupation in this country, the forests, rivers, and mountains teeming with animal life, and offering the same rich and varied fauna as the rest of Brazil, for the most part strange to an European. Among the larger animals we find the ape, ounce, wild boar, carpincho or river-hog, tatù or dasypsus, raposa and guarà of the wild dog species, quati or nasua solitaria, tamandua or myrmecophaga; among the reptiles, the rattle-snake, crocodile, surucucu and jararaca snakes, the latter very deadly, and known as trigono-cephalus, with numbers of frogs and toads. Among the fishes are—piaba, dourado, bagre, suruby, trahira, carà, &c. The dourado is of the carp species, and well known in the River Plate waters; in the estuary of Rio Grande are found crabs and other salt-water fish. The birds are in boundless variety, including cardinals, sunbirds, canaries, humming-birds, partridge, duck, turkey, ostrich, jacù, jacutinga, urubù, gaviao, pintasilgo, coleiro, prince, sabia, &c. The sunbird is called by the natives 'urutao,' from a sound which it makes, and keeps its eyes fixed steadily on the sun from early morning till sunset; it is found in the woods of the Uruguay valley, and is also known in North America. Among the insects we find silk-worms, bees, ants, and scorpions. All the domestic animals of Europe are in great abundance and thrive admirably.

The Indian tribes that were found here by the Jesuits when the country was first settled were the Minuanos and Charruas in the lower grounds, and the Tapes and Coroados in the mountains,

## PROVINCE OF RIO GRANDE. 27

all of which waged a fierce war with the Portuguese until many of the natives were converted to Christianity, and formed into seven reductions under Jesuit rule, near the valley of the Uruguay. After the expulsion of the Jesuits most of the converted tribes, as elsewhere in South America, relapsed into barbarism, but there are still numerous vestiges which show the handiwork of the natives under such masters, and the degree of advancement they had attained to. At present the remnants of the above tribes are found in a savage state among the woods of the Serra Geral or the Uruguay, from which they sometimes make incursions on the nearest farm or settlement; or else you may see a few scattered groups of 'civilised Indians' in the villages of Nonohay and San Nicolao. The number of aborigines is not known, but is relatively small. A census taken in 1814 showed the Indian population of the seven missions of Uruguay to be as follows:—

|  |  |  | Population |
|---|---|---|---|
| San Miguel | founded in | 1632 | 706 |
| San Luis Gonzaga | ,, | ,, | 1,412 |
| San Nicolao | ,, | 1627 | 1,545 |
| San Francisco Borja | ,, | 1690 | 1,424 |
| San Lorenzo | ,, | 1691 | 434 |
| San Juan Baptista | ,, | 1698 | 554 |
| San Anjo | ,, | 1707 | 320 |
|  |  |  | 6,395 |

When the inhabitants of these missions were subsequently scattered, the Government tried to form new reductions with Franciscan and other friars, but their success was very different from that of the Jesuits.

In 1860 there were six Indian villages, San Vicente, San Nicolao, Nonohay, Sta Isabel, Guarita, and Pontam, with an aggregate population of 2,107. At present there are only two, Nonohay and San Nicolao, and the inhabitants are described as naked, filthy, and squalid; the first has 590, the second 212 inhabitants. The unreduced savages of Serra Geral occasionally give annoyance to the colonists; in 1867 they murdered a German family, and carried off some children. The Coroados are one of the most savage tribes met with in Brazil, and are supposed to be descended from an ancient powerful tribe known as Goytakazes. Some of the earliest Portuguese settlers came into Rio Grande in 1680 from the neighbouring settlements of San Paulo and San Vicente. The character of the present inhabitants is observed to partake much of the Spanish nature, owing to the proximity of this province to the dominions that belonged to the crown of Spain.

The first census taken was in 1803, by Governor

Paulo Da Silva Gama, at the direction of the Portuguese Cabinet, and it showed 36,721 inhabitants, without including infants under twelve months, the troops of the line, and about 4,000 peons who had no fixed residence, but went about from one saladero to another: the returns were thus :—

| | |
|---|---:|
| Port Alegre | 3,927 |
| Viamao | 2,065 |
| Triumpho | 3,037 |
| Dos Anjos | 2,718 |
| Rio Grande | 8,390 |
| Estreito | 1,713 |
| Mostardas | 1,187 |
| Villa Principe | 3,739 |
| Sant Amaro | 1,661 |
| Taquary | 916 |
| Cachooira | 3,283 |
| San Antonio | 2,199 |
| Vaccaria | 815 |
| Arroyo | 1,041 |

In 1814 the population was found to be 70,656, made up in this manner :—

| | |
|---|---:|
| Whites | 32,300 |
| Slaves | 20,611 |
| Indians | 8,655 |
| Free coloured people | 5,399 |
| Infants under a year | 3,691 |
| | 70,656 |

During the following thirty years it doubled, but the increase was still more rapid after the close of the ten years' civil war; and, in Dec. 1862, the return showed 392,725, of whom 77,419 were slaves, or one-fifth of the total population. The districts were as follows:—

|  | Free | Slaves |
|---|---|---|
| Port Alegre | 77,872 | 17,924 |
| San Antonio | 25,875 | 5,333 |
| Rio Pardo | 30,385 | 9,467 |
| Caçapava | 15,231 | 3,285 |
| Bagé | 16,316 | 5,837 |
| Alegrete | 20,304 | 4,564 |
| Cruz Alta | 39,114 | 5,976 |
| San Borja | 17,272 | 2,396 |
| Piratiny | 24,846 | 11,266 |
| Rio Grande | 41,969 | 11,371 |
| Army, &c. | 6,122 | — |
|  | 315,306 | 77,419 |

If we allow an increase of twenty-five per cent. for the past decade it would give the present population of the province at 500,000 souls, which is rather under than over what I believe is the reality. It is more than the Republic of Uruguay can boast, and about the same as the population of the province of Buenos Ayres. The troops of the line in the various cities and frontier posts usually number 4,000 men. The national guards comprise 26,000 cavalry, 17,000 infantry, and a small battery of artillery.

The favourite occupation of the native inhabitants is raising cattle, the first estancias having been marked out in 1715, when Juan de Magalhaes came hither with a band of adventurers by order of the Governor of Santa Catharina. The killing of cattle for the exportation of hides and jerked beef also gives employment to thousands of persons in the various charqueadas or saladeros at Pelotas and elsewhere. Agriculture is almost exclusively left to the German colonists, who number about 80,000 souls, spread over forty-two colonies, chiefly in the valleys of Jacuhy, Sinos, Cahy, and Taquary. A large number of native Brazilians devote themselves to the raising of yerba-màte in the forests of the north and centre. Others act as boatmen and carriers on the numerous rivers, bringing down lumber and produce. Mining industry is in its infancy; some trifling gold-washings at Sant Antonio das Lavras, and the coal-fields of Candiota and Arroyo dos Ratos. Official papers show that a concession for digging coal was taken out so far back as 1809; the industry is now being renewed simultaneously at both the above places, and a railroad, eight miles long, will connect San Jeronimo with the Arroyo dos Ratos coal-fields. There are three shafts from 180 to 200 feet deep, and it is estimated the coal-deposits amount to 7,000,000 tons. The forests are being turned to good account by the establishment of numerous steam saw-mills on the estates of wealthy proprietors.

The great drawback is the want of roads, which paralyses the industry of the colonists, although they supply potatoes, butter, cheese, maize, farinha, &c., to Port Alegre and Rio Grande, and even export large quantities to Rio Janeyro and other distant ports. The rivers in some cases supply the want of roads; thus the Jacuhy offers 200 miles of easy traffic for the towns of Rio Pardo, Cachoeira, San Jeronymo, and Port Alegre. The last-named place being the centre of the fluvial system and capital of the province, it is proposed to draw hence three great highways; one by the Jacuhy valley to San Barja on the Uruguay; another from Port Alegre to the seaport of Desterro, which is the capital of Santa Catharina; a third by the Taquary or Cahy valleys to Cima da Serra. The river highways are navigable for steamers as follows—

|  | Miles |
| --- | --- |
| Rio Grande | 40 |
| San Gonzalo | 48 |
| Lake Mirim | 96 |
| Jaguaron | 20 |
| Lake Patos | 144 |

## PROVINCE OF RIO GRANDE.

|  | Miles |
|---|---|
| Guayba | 36 |
| Jacuhy | 192 |
| Taquary | 24 |
| Cahy | 60 |
| Sinos | 56 |
| Maquine | 44 |
| Cadea | 20 |
| Gravatahy | 20 |
| Pelotas | 20 |
| Piratinin | 24 |
| Uruguay | 336 |

There are three steamboat companies on the line between Rio Grande and Port Alegre, a distance of 240 miles; two plying between Rio Grande and Monte Video : two of Lamport and Holt's steamers every month to Rio Janeyro; and a multitude of small steamboats on the rivers above enumerated.

The various cities, towns, and villages of the province, with the date of foundation and present number of inhabitants, are as follow:—

|  | A.D. | Inhabitants |
|---|---|---|
| San Borja | 1698 | 2,000 |
| Viamao | 1741 | 400 |
| Rio Grande | 1737 | 18,000 |
| Concepcion do Arroyo | 1742 | 700 |
| Sant Antonio da Patrulha | 1760 | 1,000 |
| Rio Pardo | 1769 | 2,000 |
| Port Alegre | 1772 | 40,000 |
| Caxoeira | 1779 | 2,000 |
| Taquary | 1795 | 2,000 |
| Triumpho | 1795 | 1,500 |
| Encrucilhada | 1799 | 1,500 |

|   | A.D. | Inhabitants |
|---|---|---|
| Piratiny | 1810 | 1,800 |
| Bagè | 1812 | 2,500 |
| Pelotas | 1812 | 13,000 |
| Cangussu | 1812 | 1,800 |
| San Josè do Norte | 1820 | 800 |
| San Leopoldo | 1824 | 3,000 |
| Camaquam | 1833 | 1,200 |
| San Gabriel | 1837 | 1,800 |
| Cruz Alta | 1834 | 3,000 |
| Bocca do Monte | 1837 | 1,000 |
| Caçapava | 1833 | 1,500 |
| Baumschneitz | 1838 | 1,000 |
| San Patrico de Itaquy | 1837 | 1,500 |
| Yaguaron | 1846 | 6,000 |
| Uruguayana | 1846 | 3,000 |
| Alegrete | 1846 | 2,500 |
| Passo Fundo | 1847 | 200 |
| Sant Ana do Livramento | 1848 | 1,000 |
| San Jeronymo | 1851 | 1,000 |

The more important of these towns will be fully described in subsequent chapters. They are well provided with churches, hospitals, schools, and other public institutions. The Bishop of Port Alegre is diocesan of the province, which is divided into seventy-five parishes. There are 168 public schools, and ninety-two private ones, which are attended by 11,932 children, two-thirds boys. The hospitals and orphan asylums claim the admiration of strangers: at Port Alegre there are five hospitals, including the French, German, and Portuguese; the latter have also hospitals at Rio Grande and Pelotas. There are four fine establishments fo··

orphan girls at Port Alegre, including that of the Sisters of Charity; and another is at Pelotas. Besides the State bank at Port Alegre and the Bank of Brazil and English Bank at Rio Grande, there are branches of the Mauá Bank at Rio Grande, Port Alegre, Pelotas and Bagè. Baron Mauá is a native of this province, and has laboured much for its advancement.

The revenue and expenditure of the province are small, say a dollar a-head, or one-fourth of what the provincial budget of B. Ayres amounts to, with an equal population. The revenue averages 110,000*l.* per annum, showing a small surplus each year, viz. :—

| | |
|---|---:|
| President and staff | £3,500 |
| Provincial legislature | 3,500 |
| Bishop and clergy | 800 |
| Schools | 17,500 |
| Police | 13,500 |
| Collection of taxes | 15,000 |
| Emigrant subsidies | 5,000 |
| Conversion of Indians | 600 |
| Half-pay servants | 2,000 |
| Orphan asylums | 2,000 |
| Hospitals | 4,500 |
| Arsenal boys | 800 |
| Subsidies, &c. | 14,000 |
| Interest on public debt | 11,000 |
| Sundries | 8,000 |
| Surplus | 8,300 |
| | 110,000 |

The Imperial revenue derived from the Customhouses of Rio Grande at Port Alegre averages 350,000*l.* per annum, of which two-thirds from import duties, one-sixth from export, and the rest from other taxes.

The trade with England, Hamburg, and the United States is considerable: the value of imported merchandise is about 600,000*l.*, of which one-third is from England, an almost equal ratio from Hamburg, and the rest from France, United States, and River Plate. The value of exports may be put down at 750,000*l.*, of which one-half is to England, one-fifth to the United States, the rest to France, Portugal, and La Plata.

This does not include the coasting traffic with Rio Janeyro, Pernambuco, Bahia, and other ports of the Empire, which is quite equal to the whole of the direct foreign trade. The exports to foreign countries consist almost exclusively of hides. The exports to other parts of Brazil are largely made up of cereals from the German colonies. The port of Rio Grande represents two-thirds of the total trade of the province, and Port Alegre one-fifth, the only other market of any magnitude being Uruguayana. The first-named despatches yearly a million hides, and from 30,000 to 40,000 tons of dried beef. The

Capitania returns show that one-third of the tonnage is British, one-tenth Brazilian, and a like ratio corresponding to each of the three flags, German, Dutch, and Portuguese.

Rio Grande was the first seat of government, and was founded by Governor Silva Paes of Rio Janeyro, in 1737, who remained here two years and was succeeded by four governors, till 1763, when Rio Grande was invaded by Ceballos, and the seat of government removed to the village of Viamao in the interior, near where Port Alegre now stands. Four governors ruled at Viamao in the short interval of ten years, one of these being Colonel Sepulvedo, who was banished from Portugal for having killed a foreign officer in a duel and condemned to serve in Brazil under the assumed name of Marcelino Figueiredo, but at last obtained permission to return to Portugal, and died governor of Tras-os-Montes, in 1808 : he was the first governor at Port Alegre, having removed the seat of power thither in 1773. Eight governors sat at Port Alegre, from General Camera, who annexed Misiones in 1780, to Brigadier Daun (now Duke of Saldanha in Portugal), who refused to acknowledge the independence of Brazil and was expelled in 1822. Since then the province has been ruled by forty-two presidents, from Viscount San eopoldo to the present enlightened statesman, Homem de Mello: the only interruption was in 1835, when the civil war broke out, and President Fernandes Braga removed the seat of government to Rio Grande, while Vice-President Pereyra Ribeyro assumed power at Port Alegre. The actual President has been a staunch supporter of Viscount Rio Branco in the abolition of slavery, and his programme of government is—railways and immigration.

## II.

### CITY OF RIO GRANDE.

Rio Grande, November 13, 1871.

THE 'Camoens' entered port early this morning, and I found the city in unusual bustle owing to the inauguration of the Gas-works. Whatever side you turn you meet English engineers, some belonging to the water-works, some to the gas company, some to the Pelotas Dredge, some to the Government enterprise for deepening the Rio Grande bar: and as a natural consequence every stranger is immediately put down for an engineer. I have been asked more than once if I am for the Gas or the Water-works, and have not yet made up my mind which. The hotels are so crowded with English engineers that I should have been compelled to take up my quarters in a cockloft over M. Pascal's kitchen, had not a hospitable countryman received me with open arms and presented me with the freedom of his house.

Rio Grande at first sight is a poor-looking place, the approach for several miles from the bar being an interminable vista of sand-hills. It is a port of considerable trade, vessels of 250 tons coming to moorings alongside the shore : here you see the black peons shipping hides for England, yonder they are discharging Chilian flour from M. Video; some of these negroes are slaves, others are free and possess much money, but all are happy, good-humoured-looking fellows.

The streets are clean, irregular, well paved, and lined with houses in the Brazilian style, some four or five stories high, the fronts decorated with blue and white porcelain tiles, which saves one's eyes from the dreadful glare of Spanish whitewashed towns. The interior of the better class of houses reminds one of European comfort, but the most striking feature is the spacious dimensions of the rooms, which have, moreover, numerous windows, and are delightfully cool and agreeable. The house of Proudfoot & Co. is one of the best, situated in the Rua Pedro II., or main street; and close by is a handsome square building (with shops in the lower story) which cost 30,000*l.* sterling, and was erected last year.

Nearly in front of the Custom-house is the shop

## CITY OF RIO GRANDE.

of Messrs. Halliwell, chemists and druggists, a favourite rendezvous of strangers. The Foreign Club, with many-windowed saloons of vast size and cool temperature, looks out upon the port and lake, commanding a view of the fertile Ilha dos Marinheiros and the aquatic suburb of San José do Norte. The fruit market, as in most Brazilian towns, is well worth a visit, having abundance of fruit, vegetables, fish, &c., from Marineros Island; the market-people are mostly coloured, and one old woman is said to be owner of six slaves of her own colour; there are rows of trees through the market which give it a pleasant look. The plazas and some of the streets are also planted. Near the chief square is the Town-hall, a quadrangular building, where the municipal fathers meet; also the printing office of 'Echo do Sul,' one of the principal morning papers. This small city of 17,000 inhabitants boasts five daily papers.

There is a little theatre called '7 de Setiembre,' in honour of the anniversary of Brazilian Independence. But the finest edifice is the hospital, which is large enough for a city like Buenos Ayres. It is admirable how much the Brazilians excel in their situations for the relief of suffering humanity. The churches are small, and the three I have seen possess nothing artistic or notable.

The police and public officials are courteous, respectable, and well dressed. In fact, at every turn you see the signs of healthy administration and good government; although I cannot omit to mention that the custom-house officers left us waiting half an hour in the sun, because the 'Vista' was at his breakfast. The hotels are small and uncomfortable, but the *cuisine* is good; charges reasonable, ventilation imperfect.

Notwithstanding the sand-hills round the town, the temperature is generally cool, owing to the almost daily sea-breeze; and in winter the cold is said to be intense. A few miles inland there is luxuriant vegetation. Mr. Crawford's quinta of Arrial, nine miles distant, reminds one of the shady avenues of Aranjuez, in the desert plateau of Old Castile; it produced last season 100,000 oranges.

Numerous steamers ply to Pelotas, Porto Alegre, Yaguaron, and other ports of Lakes Patos and Merim: the finest is the 'Guayiba' (in which I leave to-day for Porto Alegre), which was built in the Clyde for Messrs. Proudfoot & Co., the great English house wherewith the trade and progress of

Rio Grande is identified. There are also two lines of steamers connecting this city with the ocean ports of Brazil and La Plata. Nothing can surpass the elegant accommodation of Messrs. Lamport & Holt's coasting steamers 'Calderon' and 'Camoens,' built specially for this trade, and carrying the Brazilian flag as mail steamers of the imperial service. During the six months they have been running, they have never yet lost a day by the Rio Grande bar, which was often so formidable to the old line of steamers as to keep them a week inside or out at sea before they durst venture over it. This bar is a great obstacle, but the Provincial Legislature is desirous of removing it. Tug-boats are kept in constant service; and once inside the bar, the port is sheltered and secure for shipping.

The principal trade is in the hands of English or Germans, but the native merchants are also intelligent, active, and well educated, some of them speaking English as fluently as ourselves, although most of them have never been outside the bar of Rio Grande. This province has produced some very remarkable men; Baron Mauá, father of Brazilian steam-navigation, was born near Pelotas; Marshal Osorio, the *preux chevalier* of the empire, comes from the same locality; and the present military governor of the city, General Salustiano, gained much distinction in the recent campaign.

There are two banks, those of Mauá & Co., which has its branches all over Brazil and the River Plate, and the London and Brazilian, established some four years ago. There are many wealthy capitalists here, and money is held as cheap as in the River Plate; the currency is almost exclusively paper, at a discount of ten per cent., which may be regarded as the fixed rate. Interest rules about twelve per cent. per annum, but some people prefer building for an investment.

The place will be much improved when it possesses water-supply and gas. The contractors, Messrs. Upward & Illingworth, who arrived here some four months ago, representing the San Pedro Brazilian Gas Company (limited), made the preliminary arrangements with the promptitude characteristic of our countrymen, and the streets were opened to-day at noon in front of the Custom-house to put down the first pipes. The municipal and other authorities were present, besides a large number of citizens, the editors of the local papers, and the chief English and German residents. General Salustiano, Colonel Ran-

## CITY OF RIO GRANDE.

gel, and the staff-officers of the garrison were in full uniform, the 7th battalion of the Line forming a guard of honour, and the military band playing national airs. An Irish sub-contractor with a gang of workmen deposited the pipes, and Mr. Upward advancing, presented a silver mallet to Don Francisco Jose Cunha, mayor of the city, who gave the pipes two strokes with the mallet and declared the works duly begun.

Mr. Upward addressed the Mayor in English as follows :—

'Most worshipful mayor and city councillors of Rio Grande, right worthy representatives of this flourishing population, I come on behalf of the San Pedro Brazilian Gas Company to congratulate you on this happy occasion of laying down the first pipes to light your city with gas. I trust that before long, your streets, squares, and buildings will be illuminated, and that this great improvement will be, as it is elsewhere, the forerunner of such additional comfort and progress as to insure the prosperity and advancement of Rio Grande. The directors will spare no efforts in the matter, counting on the decided assistance of the Brazilian Government.'

The Mayor replied—'Illustrious Senhor Upward, I salute you as the distinguished engineer of the San Pedro Gas Company. The town council accept your invitation with pleasure, to assist at the inauguration of these works under your able direction, and all my fellow-citizens rejoice with me at the prospect of so great an improvement as lighting our town with gas. May Divine Providence protect the company and pour his choicest blessings on this our native city.!'

Cheers of 'Long live Dom Pedro,' 'Viva Brazil,' 'Viva la Compagnia Ingleza,' &c. rent the air, simultaneous with rockets and strains of martial music, amid which the meeting dispersed, and some of the English strangers remarked that it looked irresistibly ludicrous to see so many umbrellas on a fine sunny day; but the heat is already sufficient to call for such shelter. In the afternoon Mr. Upward left by mail-steamer 'Camoens' for Rio Janeyro *en route* for Europe, and was accompanied aboard by the most of the leading citizens, Mr. Consul Callendar, and others. I had the pleasure of making the acquaintance of the Consul, who is much esteemed here, and of most of the foreign residents.

The city of Rio Grande has little attraction for an idle visitor, but is the chief commercial em-

## CITY OF RIO GRANDE. 47

porium in these waters. I am told that Port Alegre, 20 hours or 180 miles distant by water, is a terrestrial paradise, in the midst of the most delightful scenery; it has a larger population than this city, and is the residence of the chief authorities as well as of numerous German merchants.

Before closing my remarks on Rio Grande, I may observe that the place is proverbially healthy. Last evening I visited the English and native cemeteries, and chanced to meet the Town Clerk, Mr. Saa, a polished gentleman, who speaks English fluently, and who assures me that often a day or two passes without a single interment, although the average mortality for a place of 17,000 souls might be expected to range at 12 weekly. The only English names I noticed were Mr. Thomas Messiter, who died in 1860, aged 68 years, and Mr. Wm. M'Crae in 1862, aged 39 years. Both cemeteries are well kept. The land side of the city is protected by a strong wall with bastions and demi-lunes pierced by two gates, but in some places the sand has risen to a level with the top of the battlements. Wild dogs burrow in the sand and live there.

Beturning from the cemetery you pass the barrack, which holds 300 cavalry, and the Portuguese Hospital of Beneficencia. The Caridad, or city hospital, is a massive structure on the water's edge, of which I have already spoken. There are three public and as many private schools, but many people send their children to be educated at Rio Janeyro or elsewhere.

Strangers coming to Rio Grande should procure a letter of introduction to Messrs. Proudfoot & Co. as their best passport, for under the protection of Mr. Crawford they can be wanting in neither advice nor assistance.

## III.

### *RIO GRANDE TO PORT ALEGRE.*

THE immense inland sea known as Lagoa dos Patos, nearly 200 miles across, is navigated by numerous steamers plying between Rio Grande, Pelotas, Port Alegre, Yaguaron, and other ports of the interior. The chief trade is between Rio Grande and Port Alegre, which maintains three lines of steamers, affording bi-weekly communication. I took my passage in the 'Guayiba,' the finest vessel in these waters. We had over forty first-class passengers, and the accommodations were admirable, but the fare (twenty-five milreis or fifty shillings) seemed to me very high, and I am not surprised to hear that she has already given a handsome dividend. The engines are on the compound system of high and low pressure, burning only about four tons of coal daily.

We left our moorings at the company's wharf at twelve o'clock sharp, and as we bent away northwards by a circuitous route to avoid sand-banks, a slight shower of rain fell, which served with the light sea-breeze to cool the atmosphere. On the north shore, right in front of Rio Grande, is Mr. Proudfoot's farm of Coqueruto, where he made several efforts to plant cotton some seven or eight years ago, laying down considerable tracts of land, and putting up cotton-jins and machinery; but although the soil seemed suitable and the plants came up healthy and vigorous, they would not ripen in season, and the scheme had to be abandoned. The farm is now used for growing market produce, and managed by a Scotchman. Mr. Proudfoot has two other farms in the neighbourhood; in fact, wherever you turn you hear or see evident signs of the energy and enterprise of this representative man, one of the earliest foreigners who developed the resources of this part of Brazil, and who even now, while enjoying the fruits of a princely fortune in his native hills of Scotland, has his attention so fixed upon the progress of these countries, that every year he embarks in some new enterprise of steam-boats, telegraphs, railways, gas, &c., to aid in the march of progress.

The desolate hamlet of San José de Norte is

half buried in the sand-hills facing the port of Rio Grande, and sailing-boats make the run across in half an hour. We pass near enough to see that most of the houses appear untenanted, except some on the beach, one of which bears the legend, 'English ship store.' A good-sized church is in the background, but some day I fear a sand-slip will overthrow the place. One of the passengers remarks that these arid sands and white houses remind him of Suez, which is about the most inhospitable place known; yet we are told that half an hour's ride from San José takes you into a pleasant country where there is plenty of shooting, and here and there a chacra or farmhouse.

Passing a lighthouse and some cottages, we enter the Lagoa dos Patos, and see a magnificent sheet of fresh water without other land on the horizon than the Sierras of Pelotas. At the foot of those hills an Irish colony was established some twenty years ago, but it proved a failure; whether owing to the country, or the colonists themselves, I will not venture to say. Some of the settlers remained only a few months, alleging that they could not eat 'sawdust,' as they called the fariña; others removed to Buenos Ayres after a trial of one or two seasons, and a stray vestige of the colony alone remains.

Our passengers on board are mostly Germans, for Port Alegre is in a manner a German settlement, the first colony having been fixed there in 1825, and now there are 60,000 Germans in the province. They never think of returning to Europe, but become, like the Irish in North America and Buenos Ayres, permanent settlers in their adopted home. Still they preserve the warmest recollections of the Fatherland, and in language, sentiment, and traditions are as true to their native country as if only travellers in a strange land. As the sun was setting behind the Pelotas range, one of the passengers struck up the 'Wacht am Rhein,' and the broad waters of the lake echoed to the chorus—

> Fest steht und treu
> Die Wacht am Rhein.

Memories of the Fatherland, traditions of the Rhine, stories from the recent battle-fields whiled away the hours of twilight, and the 'young May moon' was far on her midnight course ere we retired to sleep. Before sunrise I was again on deck to see the panorama of Itapoa, where the estuary of Guayiba communicates with the great lake. Hills covered with forest come down on either side, leaving only a narrow channel, where the lighthouse of Itapoa stands. To the left is the rounded promontory of Barba Negra, where the old lighthouse stood. I may observe that the coasts of this lake have several lighthouses, and some of the narrow channels are regularly buoyed.

The Guayiba estuary is formed of four rivers— the Tacahuy, Lacuhy, Sinos, and Gravitahy; the whole, as seen from a neighbouring hill, resemble a man's hand, for which it is called Viamao. Nothing can be imagined more picturesque and delightful than the ranges of wooded hills surrounding this second lake, the banks of which are lined with farms and country-houses nestling in luxuriant foliage, and the shadows thrown by the clouds chase each other from hill to hill, while the alternations of light and dark green, the murmur of waters gently breaking on the shore, and the distant view of Port Alegre crowning yonder hill, form a picture full of charm and varied attraction. Arriving within cannon-shot, we reach Pedras Blancas, where the powder-magazine is kept, an island of immense loose stones, piled one on another so fantastically, that you would fancy a person could push some of them down, though weighing several tons each. The city and port now unfold themselves before us in a picture of surpassing loveliness.

## IV.

### PORT ALEGRE.

NONE can have an idea what a paradise this place is. I have never seen anything so charming as the scenery by land and water all around.

On Wednesday we rode out by Baron D'Ornano's villa to a hill commanding the plain of Viamon, Sierras, and the wood of Matto-grosso; and yesterday Mr. Coulborn, contractor for dredges, &c., took us in his steam-launch up the Jacuhy.

To-morrow there is another excursion fifty miles by water, and on Tuesday we start for the Colonies; the nearest, San Leopoldo, is forty miles distant, and Messrs. Smith, Sawers, Turner, &c., are now making the railway from this city.

Port Alegre is a thriving place, and since the invasion by English engineers within the last few months the change is marvellous. The gas-works were inaugurated last week, and when the railway and other works are completed, it will go ahead very fast. A concession is granted for a railway hence to Sta. Catalina (200 miles), to have a new and better port than Rio Grande.

This city has double the population of Rio Grande, probably 40,000 inhabitants, several fine shops, a splendid theâtre, treasury, townhall, arsenal, college, &c. The Brazilian and Portuguese hospitals, German clubs, cathedral, plazas, &c. are also very fine. The water supply is admirable; fountains play in the streets, and every house has pipe-water service, by mains brought six miles from the mountains, and laid down in 1805 by a French contractor. The concessionaire of the gas is Baron D'Ornano, a Corsican related to the Bonaparte and Colonna families, and late French Consul here, who sold his concession in London. Delightful country-houses surround the city, the finest being those of Sor. Inocencio, manager of the Mauá Bank, Sor. Lisboa, an army contractor, Baron Gravitahy (whose house was the emperor's residence during his stay here), and numerous others.

Messrs. Gardner Brothers have established a foundry where they make saw-mills, coffee-mills,

## PORT ALEGRE.

&c., for the fazendas in the interior. Messrs. Armishaw have a large English house of business, and the other residents are Messrs. Dillon, Thompson, Maguire, &c.

The wonder of the province are the German colonies, summing up 60,000 people, who have converted virgin forests into waving corn-fields, interspersed with neat farm-houses and all the appliances of agricultural life: the first, San Leopoldo, was founded in 1825, and there are now many similar; there are three newspapers published in German, and the advancement of the country is mainly due to these industrious settlers. Even the negroes often talk German; in fact it is a German principality in the heart of the Brazilian Empire.

The Rio Grandenses are the nicest Brazilians I have met with, very kind and obliging to strangers, many of them talking English and French fluently. The signs of good government and administration are visible on all sides; the arsenal, city prison, &c. resemble what you would look for in England.

But that the steamer goes to-day I could write whole pages about this interesting and delightful place. In my excursions on horseback or steamer, Messrs. Coulborn, MacGinity, Armishaw, Archer, &c. have kindly promised to accompany me. Mr. Coulborn is M.A. of Oxford. I have been exceedingly fortunate to fall in with such pleasant companions.

## V.

### THE SUBURBS OF PORT ALEGRE.

EXCURSIONS by land or water in the vicinity of this city reveal such a variety of enchanting scenery that one might spend months here without satiety, visiting every day some new point of beauty, for the panorama of Port Alegre is like a kaleidoscope with so many changes of lovely vistas. Last Wednesday I rode out with some friends towards the Caixa de Agua or reservoir, a few miles from town. The moment we passed the Caridad Hospital we got a view of the Guayiba valley and lake, and the splendid woodland scenery stretching away to Dos Irmaos and San Leopoldo. The country-houses in the outskirts are surrounded with gardens and orange-groves. The roads are good, but sometimes steep, with hedgerows on either side as in England. Green lanes, park-like wood and meadow, murmuring streams, tall palms, and at intervals a wood-cutter's rude waggon or a troop of mules from the mountain; these are the characteristics of the country, but now and then you instinctively halt your horse to gaze upon the lovely landscape, in which the five rivers, like bands of silver, intersect the wooded valleys and enhance the tropical vegetation around.

The sun was setting as we gained the ridge overlooking Matto-Grosso, a thick forest which was much infested with robbers a dozen years ago. Returning towards the city we passed the country-houses of sundry noble families, and alighted at that of Baron D'Ornano, a Corsican, who received us with great courtesy: the Baron is a good linguist and speaks in high terms of the scenery and natural resources of this province, all of which he has travelled over during a residence of fifteen years. He showed us the records of his family for 1,200 years, and added that the long line ended with himself: he lives in an unfinished chateau that looks like the Castle of Otranto, some rude boards answering for the hall-door; and the chapel wing being used for out-offices: the owner died before finishing the structure and left his family but scanty resources. The ball-room and dining-hall are splendid apartments, and from the turrets is obtained an extensive view. The Baron lives with a few servants and a little blue-eyed boy whom he has adopted.

On Thursday Mr. Coulborn invited me with a few other friends to an excursion in his little steam-yacht up the River Dos Sinos. The day was fine, with a cool breeze over the lake, and as we awoke the echoes of the Guayiba we had occasion to admire a long coast-line of elegant country-houses, among which that of Sor. Lisboa, a contractor during the late war, was remarkable for architectural taste. The line of railway to San Leopoldo and New Hamburg will run along this coast-line. Yonder is a neat villa with gardens in front; it is a second orphan asylum (besides Sta. Theresa) and accommodates forty little girls. The orange-trees are laden with fruit, and the negroes sing at their work as we pass. Ascending the Sinos we enter upon beautiful river scenery, the woods forming fantastic vistas and every shade of foliage from golden to dark green. At times we come upon cottages with a row of palms in front, or nestling in orange-groves, the children playing on the green sward, forgetful of alligators. Last year a German gardener who lived hereabout lost a little boy of seven years old, a yacaré coming up from the river and carrying off the child before the distracted parents could run to its rescue. Large square-built villas are passed as we ascend, for some of these places are the property of wealthy 'fazendeiros.' At last we arrive at a bend of the river which discloses a handsome country-house and plantations, the residence of D. Bento Cyrio, an Italian baker, some forty years a resident of Port Alegre, where he amassed a large fortune and gained the reputation of a model citizen for honesty and persevering labour; he now lives with his numerous family in baronial affluence on his estate, and this is a favourite place for pic-nics by water.

We went some miles higher, meeting a steamer full of passengers from San Leopoldo and several sailing craft laden with lumber or other produce. By a circuitous route through the islands we got into the River Jacuhy, and returned this way to the city, coming out near the old powder-magazine in the islands.

To form a proper idea of the city we steamed round to the southern bay in direction of Santa Theresa. Looking towards the hill of Santa

Anna, where the citizens often go on holidays, we see the chapel of Menino Deos or the Infant Saviour, famed for the religious festivities celebrated here every Christmas, and lasting some twenty days. Nearer town is the seat of the late Baron Gravitahy, who earned his title in the war of Independence; the Emperor resided here in 1845, when he first visited this province; the architecture and plantations are the result of combined wealth and taste. Close by is the Villa of Sor. Inocencio, manager of the Mauá branch-bank; other houses and gardens fill up the background. We double the extreme west point, on which the prison stands, and land at the Custom House, after a delightful day's travel. The steam-yacht is a miniature vessel, the first of its size on the combined principle of high and low pressure, and goes easily twelve miles an hour (with the current we made fourteen), while the whole amount of coal for a day's excursion would fit in a small market basket; she requires only one man to mind the engine and another to steer, and can carry a dozen passengers or more. Mr. Coulborn says the cost, placed in South America, is about 500*l*., and indeed nothing can be imagined more suitable for a private family for pleasure parties. I forgot to mention that amongst our company was the editor of the 'Rio Grandense,' Mr. Berlink, a gentleman of varied information and a good French scholar.

Another pleasant ride from town is to the chapel of Menino Deos, overlooking the southern bay of the Guayiba estuary. The view at early morning is delightful, the mists slowly rising from the water, over which the shadows of the clouds sweep in fantastic forms, while the rising sun shines upon the white cottages embosomed in luxuriant vegetation, and the wooded hills behind seem to shut out all cares of the exterior world. It is only perhaps in the golden bay of Palermo, or from the hill which commands the 'lower lake' of Killarney, that such an atmosphere of repose, blended with all that is most beautiful to the eye, steals over the enraptured senses and hushes the very pulsations of your heart in mute admiration. If you ascend to Morro do Cristales or Belen you will also find lovely panoramas, as indeed you will from any commanding point in this earthly paradise.

## VI.

### ENGLISH ENTERPRISES IN PORT ALEGRE.

RAILWAYS, dredges, gas-works, coal-mines, foundries, &c. are the order of the day, all new enterprises in the hands of English engineers, the necessary capital in most cases being also raised in England. It is easy to predict a great and rapid development of industry in this part of the Brazils, the most favoured in soil and climate of all the vast empire.

The eminent engineers, Messrs. Sawer and Turner, whose names are already favourably known in connection with the Bahia and Pernambuco lines, are constructing the New Hamburg Railway, which will open up an important trade between the German colonies and this city, which at present maintains three distinct lines of steamers, the distance by land being twenty-eight miles. When the first steamer was put on, a few years ago, it was doubted whether it would prove a paying business, but before long a second was started, and the trade so much increased that further competition sprang up, and now the daily steam traffic is well supported. The originator of the New Hamburg Railway is Mr. John MacGinity, an old Scotch resident, who has a hand in every enterprise of progress in and about Port Alegre; he began life in Rio Janeyro as overseer of a department of Mauá's iron-works, and has since held responsible posts under the Brazilian Government in connection with steam-boats and machinery, besides taking contracts in construction of the prison, arsenal, &c. of this city, making surveys of the adjacent lakes and rivers, and using every effort to push forward the San Jeronimo coal-mines. Mr. MacGinity returned from England a few months since and is now superintendent of the railway works; he is also United States' Vice-Consul and agent for several English firms and insurance offices. He is a large landed proprietor, and offers free land-grants of 100 acres to each settler, on lands situate between two of the most flourishing German colonies.

The prospectus of the New Hamburg Railway, published at London last January, shows the capital of the Company at 292,500*l.* sterling, in shares of

20*l.* each, with a guarantee of 5 per cent. for sixty years from the Government of Rio Grande. The directors comprise the Brazilian Minister in London, Lord Claude Hamilton, Messrs. W. Austin, F. Furrell, Captain Rennie, and G. Steward. The engineer-in-chief is Mr. James Brunlees, whose representative here is Mr. Cleary, a gentleman of long experience in Brazil. The contractors, Messrs. John Watson and John Bevan Smith, have agreed to construct the line for 280,000*l.* sterling, or 10,000*l.* a mile, of which they take one-third payment in ordinary shares. This will be the cheapest line ever made in the Brazils, the San Paulo having cost 24,000*l.* a mile, and others even more; as the San Paulo is now yielding $5\frac{1}{2}$ per cent., it may be predicted that the New Hamburg line will give more than double. This is the more probable when we see the steam-boat companies to San Leopoldo and Rio Grande give in many cases regular dividends of 30 to 60 per cent. per annum. The Government reserves the right of purchasing the line at the expiration of thirty years. The company's privilege prevents any other line being constructed within twenty miles. It cannot be doubted that the railway will tap a rich and increasing trade, the number of German colonists being estimated at forty thousand, or nearly half the population of the department of Port Alegre. Besides grain and vegetables the colonies produce tobacco, butter, pork, &c.; and the settlers are so much pleased with the genial climate and well-ordered mode of Brazilian administration, which gives them security, tranquillity, and free land-grants, that they never return to Europe, but fix all their interests in the land of their adoption. The railway will certainly give a great stimulus to the colonies and a good return to the shareholders; the cost of construction is comparatively low, seeing the mountains, rivers, &c. to be passed; in some cases the cane-brakes are so thick that it is a work of some days to cut a passage through. The scenery along the route is magnificent.

The Government of Rio Grande, being sensible of the immense importance of facilitating commerce by clearing away bars and sandbanks between this port and Rio Grande, and deepening the river of Guayiba and its five grand tributaries, have just got out from the Clyde two powerful dredges and a steam tug. The former are being put in working order by Mr. Coulborn, the constructor, who came hither in person to do so.

These dredges are independent of two others (smaller) which arrived this week at Rio Grande for Mr. Albert Smith, to clear away the bar at Pelotas, besides others used for deepening the Bay of Rio Grande. Mr. Coulborn's dredges are adapted to raise each 300 tons an hour; they are 50 horse-power nominal, or 250 effective, and may be also used as screw steamers, the engines being on Elder's principle of high and low pressure combined, which makes an important saving in coal, each of these dredges consuming only $4\frac{3}{4}$ tons in twenty-four hours. The merit of this invention of the 'combined system' is due to a Swedish engineer named Wolff. Mr. Coulborn's dredges steamed out from England to this port in fifty-three days, encountering dreadful weather; strange to say, they sighted each other only once, entering St. Vincento within half an hour, arriving off Rio Grande at a difference of only two hours. The firm of Henderson, Coulborn, & Co., of Renfrew, is one of the greatest on the Clyde, the workshops covering $18\frac{1}{2}$ acres, and employing over two thousand men; at present they have fourteen steamers building, with an aggregate tonnage of 17,000 tons, and 6,000 horse-power, representing a value of a million and a quarter sterling; the establishment was founded by John Henderson & Co. in 1850. Mr. Coulborn is a young man, little over thirty, and not only a clever engineer, but a good scholar, having taken M.A. and honours at Oxford. His father-in-law, the new Provost of Glasgow, is well known in that city for his munificence, having given 10,000*l*. for the new Glasgow Library. Mr. Coulborn has built some steamers for the Rio Janeyro and Corrientes trade, and intends visiting the River Plate next month, before returning home.

We lately witnessed the inauguration of the gas-works for this city by Messrs. Upward & Illingworth, who are contractors for the Company formed in England to light Port Alegre, Pelotas, and Rio Grande, the concession for which was taken out three years ago by Baron d'Ornano. The works at Rio Grande were inaugurated at the same time, and the lighting of these cities with gas will be an incalculable improvement, and probably give results as advantageous as in towns of even smaller population, such as Rosario de Santa Fé.

The coal-fields of Candiota, so much spoken of by Messrs. Nathaniel Plant and G. Law, and to which a railway is projected, are said to be much inferior to those of San Jeronimo or Arroyo de las Ratas, for which a concession obtained by Mr. Johnson hss been recently disposed of in London. Mr. Plant has also arranged respecting the Candiota mines with the banking house of Bischoffsheim & Co.

Messrs. Gardner Brothers have just established, close to the Arsenal, an English foundry, which promises to do a great and profitable business, owing to the demand for machinery in the 'fazendas' of coffee, &c. in the interior. Although only two months working, they are already putting up a saw-mill for Don Leonardo Macedonio, of Caxoeira, 200 miles inland, and a coffee-grinder and saw-mill for Messrs. Fontoura & Mariante, at Taquary, 100 miles distant, besides a brickmaking machine and other works elsewhere. At the foundry I observed a shearing and punching machine, by Craig & Donald, of Glasgow, a screwcutter, Shields' patent fan, &c., the whole driven by a six horse-power engine of Marshall & Co., of Gainsborough. Most of the workmen are English, with native apprentices. This foundry is sure to do a great business, and will be most useful for the increasing steam-boat traffic.

## VII.

### THE NEW HAMBURG RAILWAY.

THIS will be the first railway constructed in the province of Rio Grande, and seems destined to be the main trunk from which other lines will branch out towards the Atlantic and the Uruguay.

The distance from Port Alegre to San Leopoldo by rail will be only 22 miles, or half the present route by water, and hence to New Hamburg is almost 6 miles, making the entire length 28 miles; the cost of construction will be unprecedentedly low (10,000*l*. per mile), the narrow gauge of 42 inches being adopted, as best suited for a mountainous country with light traffic. There are some engineering difficulties to be overcome, three rivers to be crossed, the Sapocaia range of mountains to be traversed, some woods and cane-brakes to be cleared, and an embankment to be formed along that part of the Guayiba at the foot of the city of Port Alegre. None of these, however, can be con-

## THE NEW HAMBURG RAILWAY. 73

sidered formidable, and although the bridges are designed for a double line, the biggest of them will hardly cost 10,000*l*.

About 5 miles from Port Alegre occurs the first bridge, crossing the Rio Gravitahy, with a central span of 80 feet, and two others of 48 each, in all 176 feet. It will have longitudinal wrought-iron girders on cast-iron piers with stone abutments, the height of the bridge being 5 feet over flood level. There are several culverts of much cost and labour, but the alleged swamp, which was the bugbear of the line, turns out harmless and easy to cross. At Sapocaia there is another iron bridge, with a span of 30 feet. The greatest work on the line will be the Sinos bridge at San Leopoldo, *en route* for New Hamburg, half a mile above the former town : it will have 7 spans, the longest of 60 feet, in all 244 feet, the river-spans constructed the same as the Gravitahy, the iron-work weighing 250 tons; it will be 15 feet over ordinary water-level. As I have said above, all these bridges are to be for a double line, though at present the railway will be laid down a single one.

The line is straight for more than half its entire length, the remaining portion being a series of curves, but generally so easy (1,200 to 1,500 feet radius) as to give no anxiety. The sharpest is 819 feet radius, which in England would be thought tolerably easy. It is necessary to make this sinuous route in order to avoid the hills, which must otherwise be either ascended or tunneled. The line crosses the Sapocaia range at its lowest pass, $2\frac{1}{2}$ miles from San Leopoldo, and here of course occurs the greatest incline—1 in 50— which is much less than found in England, where there are some even of 1 in 30. The ascent from the Port Alegre side stretches over 1,000 yards, and the descent towards San Leopoldo 1,200 yards, the maximum height attained being 150 feet over the San Leopoldo station.

The deepest cutting is 29 feet, the deepest bank 30. The sleepers employed are of one or other of the ten hard woods of the country already enumerated. At a place called Steinkopf is found a serviceable red sandstone, of which the abutments of the bridges and other works will be composed. The line will traverse, besides jungle and forest, a number of German farms, the prettiest of which is Spiegelberg, close to San Leopoldo. The contractors expect to open the line thus far in twelve or eighteen months.

Messrs. Watson & Bevan Smith are also in

treaty with the Municipality of San Leopoldo for an iron road bridge over the Sinos river in front of the town, which would cost about 10,000*l*. having 3 spans of 93 feet each. The Piratiny bridge, not much larger, cost nearly four times that sum.

Mr. John MacGinity has published an interesting and minute map of the colonies and that portion of the Province which the present railway must open upon its projected prolongation from New Hamburg to Caxoeira and Uruguayana, a distance of nearly 300 miles, to be completed in annual sections over a period of about ten years.

As it is supposed, with good reason, that the traffic between New Hamburg and Port Alegre will pay a handsome dividend to the shareholders (by taking up the present remunerative trade which maintains three lines of steamers), it is intended after the first year to ask the Government to transfer the 7 per cent. guarantee to a prolonged line to Taquary, *viâ* Port Guimaraens, and so on successively to Rio Pardo, Caxoeira, St. Angelo, Santa Maria, San Pedro, San Vicente, San Francisco, Assis, Alegrete, and Uruguayana. These sections (except the last two, which are very long) average 25 miles each, passing through towns and agricultural districts of great importance. The statistical returns show that most of the districts settled by colonists have a regular increase of 20 per cent. every year over the revenues of the preceding one.

Cheap, narrow-gauge railways can be made along the entire route at the cost of the New Hamburg line (10,000*l*. per mile) ; and as the Government will always be ready to devote 30,000*l*. per annum for subsidy or guarantee, this can be put forward every year for a new section according as the previous ones become self-supporting.

Another projected railway of great importance is that traced out from Port Alegre to Torres, on the Atlantic, in the Province of Santa Catalina, a distance of nearly 100 miles : this would cost 1,000,000*l*. sterling, and the harbour works at Torres are estimated by the engineers at half that sum. It would have the effect of opening up a trade at present too remote from the port of the Rio Grande.

The advancement of the Province of Rio Grande is of course mainly due to its German colonists, who have earned for it the name of ' Granary of the Brazilian Empire.' Its finances meantime are so flourishing that last year it had a surplus of 17,600*l.* sterling, and being unburthened with any debt, it can devote every energy to the furtherance of railways, which are destined to increase the public and private wealth in a remarkable degree.

## VIII.

### THE COAL-FIELDS OF SAN JERONIMO.

'On Sunday morning we set out in Mr. Coulborn's steam-yacht from San Jeronimo, a village some sixty miles up the Jacuhy, at the mouth of its tributary the Taquary. At short distances along the route we saw farmers' and country-houses, indicating a thicker population than in the River Plate countries, and the inhabitants seeming to enjoy a comparative affluence. We met several craft with large square sails coming down stream, laden with timber or castor-oil nuts; the boatmen were in all cases natives, and sometimes had their wives and families aboard. There is nothing different from the scenery of wood and water already described of the Sinos, the first place of note being a charqueda, or saladero, near the mouth of the Arroyo dos Ratos, after which we pass the ruined mansion of the Alves family which was bombarded during the Garibaldi wars and has never been restored. After six hours' steaming we sighted San Jeronimo and Triumfo, two villages on opposite sides of the river. The latter, on the right, is older than Port Alegre, and was of some. importance in the last century; it presents a handsome appearance, crowning the hill-side with a twin-turreted church in the centre and several well-built houses.

We land at San Jeronimo, on the left, as this is the nearest point to the fields, and find it a straggling place of 800 or 900 inhabitants. An old Welshman, named Thomas Jones, gives us a cordial welcome, and prevails on us to proceed to his house on the top of the hill, about a mile off. On the route we fall in with Major Marcos, an old Brazilian officer, who speaks French, and offers his services in any way he can be useful. We halt at a tavern kept by a German, and find a crowd of fifty persons, Germans, Brazilians, negroes, &c., engaged in a brutal cock-fight. A little farther we come to an extensive factory belonging to M. Daixon, a Frenchman, who carries on the whole yerba trade of the district, employing a great number of people. The factory being closed, and the villagers amusing themselves, we called to pay a visit to the Frenchman, who received us very kindly, and talked about the coal-fields, yerba, &c. I learn from Major Marcos that M. Daixon was a hatter, and came here some fifteen years ago, but instead of following his trade, he got into partnership with a French merchant of Rio Grande, who gave him funds to start this business, now the sole trade and support of San Jeronimo: it has proved highly lucrative, and M. Daixon is reputed to be worth over 30,000*l.* sterling.

Arriving at Mr. Jones's cottage we rested under the shade of his orange-trees till dinner was ready: he is the only Englishman in the village, and has resided here twenty years. There are, however, some Welsh and Irish families ten miles inland, who were formerly occupied in the coal-fields before they stopped working. A coal-wharf still exists at San Jeronimo, where the steamers used to take in their supply. Efforts were made by Mr. MacGinity and his friends to pump out the water which flooded the mines, but owing to the want of proper miners the works had to be abandoned. Mr. Johnson, a Cornishman of some experience, has obtained a new concession and prevailed on parties in England to advance him money for another trial, with which purpose he has just arrived in Rio Janeyro to be followed by a staff of miners. These mines, usually called of Arroyo dos Ratos, must not be confounded with those of Candiota for which Mr. Nathaniel Plant is concessionaire.

On Monday morning we were up before sunrise to start for the coal-fields, eight or ten miles inland. Major Marcos kindly lent us a couple of horses. Before setting out we had occasion to admire the splendid view from Mr. Jones's door, looking down at the meeting of the waters of the Jacuhy and Taquary, nearly a mile wide. We were all well mounted, our party comprising Messrs. Bevan Smith, Sawer, MacGinity, Jones, Coulborn, and myself. The country was undulating, almost bare of timber, and thickly settled, our road lying across a high range of hills.

After two hours' ride we got sight of the coal district, sloping down from a hill-range to a wooded valley; and we halted at the house of a Welshman named Davis, whose wife expressed great joy to see us. Her husband was away near Pelotas. The house was neat, though poor; and Mrs. Davis told us of a series of misfortunes which had befallen them since their arrival, eighteen years ago. Her eldest boy, with two others of an Irish family, was blown up in a powder explosion near the works more than ten years ago. At another time her house was burnt down, and all the family stock of books, clothing, &c. consumed. Again, when the mines stopped working they were thrown out of employment, and ever since eked out a living by raising vegetables. Last year the poor woman tried her hand with a small grocery shop; but the natives, who were her customers, proved so dilatory in their cash payments that she had to close the door. Her children and grand-children had the bright eyes and flaxen hair of Britain, but no other language than Portuguese, although I believe they understood a little of what they heard in English or in the old Erse tongue of their parents. I observed a Welsh bible and some family portraits, which they had saved from the fire; and it was pleasant to see how the old woman's eyes brightened when we spoke of the old land, to which her heart still yearned as when she first left its shores, although she can hardly entertain a hope of ever again seeing her native hills. She told us that another Welsh family lived in the district, as also an Irishman named Peter Logan; and another, Patrick Garraghan, on the other side of Arroyo dos Ratos. I thought to myself, how hard the lot of these folks, after twenty years' separation from their country-people spent in persevering labour, in comparison with the flourishing condition of the Irish sheep-farmers in Buenos Ayres!

Leaving Mr. Davis's cottage, we proceeded to the mines, where pieces of machinery were lying about near the abandoned works. I picked up samples of the coal, which seemed to me very slaty; but it is said to answer when mixed with a better description. I am glad to say that Mr. MacGinity yesterday prevailed on the President to subscribe for 10,000*l.* in shares. As yet it is premature to descant on the immense advantages which these coal-fields may yield to Brazil and to the commerce of this part of South America.

It seems that Messrs. Johnson and Moura have sold their interest for 30,000*l.*, the new Company being called 'Imperial Brazilian Collieries, Limited,' capital 100,000*l.* The concession is for thirty years, and it is proposed to raise 300 tons a day, the present seam being 4 feet 8 inches thick, and estimated at 6,000,000 tons. This coal took a prize at the Paris Exhibition. A tramway will be laid down to San Jeronimo, and Johnson obliges himself to place the coal on board in that port at seven shillings a ton, which the Company will sell at twenty-four shillings at Port Alegre, whereas English coal costs sixty shillings.

## IX.

### *EXCURSION TO SAN LEOPOLDO.*

On Friday morning we left Port Alegre in the steamer 'Balastraca,' the oldest on the line. Ascending the Rio dos Sinos we soon began to feel the sun very hot, the thick woods on either side excluding the breeze, which moreover was from the north and came on us at intervals like a puff of the Sirocco. The captain of the steamer was a German, and treated us to a breakfast of trout and roast-beef, the former quite as good as what Gil Blas speaks of in his travels.

About twenty miles from Port Alegre, we passed the charming fazenda of Bento Cyrio, and higher up came to a place where they were making bricks. The river has innumerable bends, the scenery being a continued luxuriance of vegetation which at last almost wearies you. Foliage of every shade, beautifully blended, forest openings here and there, umbrageous trees like sycamores, wild cane-brakes that suggest tiger-jungles, tapering palms, and the lofty 'timba-uva' with orchids and other parasites in its highest branches; all these, interspersed with wood-cutters' huts, hedges of rhododendron, canoes with children fishing, and various kinds of water-fowl, make up the picture of all or any of these rivers. Sometimes you come on a clump of burned trees where the negroes have begun clearing a patch of ground. In many places the banks of the river have given way and large forest trees fallen into the stream, their trunks or branches often sticking out in the middle of the current, which must make night travelling very dangerous. It would be easy for the Government to employ a small steamer to drag away these snags and clear the rivers.

The high-water mark of the flood-tides is observable on the cottages that we pass, some 8 feet over the present level. The current is about 2 to 3 miles an hour. Most of the wood that lines the river-side is said to be comparatively valueless, but the Province of Rio Grande can boast at least ten good qualities of timber, chiefly hard wood, viz. ipé, black canella, cangerana, cocao, lauro, tarama, cabri-uva, tajuba, angico and grapiapuño, of which the railway sleepers are made.

The sportsman would find abundance of game in all variety, from tigers to water-hens, and the follower of Isaac Walton might open up new kingdoms in the piscatorial world, for the rivers teem with the finny tribe, and Professor Agassiz reports two thousand new kinds of fish as proper to Brazilian waters. Of amphibious animals the yacaré has a coat said to be impervious to rifle-ball, and the best chance of shooting him is when he opens his ponderous red jaws to yawn, as he basks in the sun; there is also a kind of river-hog called capibari, not different from the carpincho of Argentine waters; lizards of great size are also seen; these animals seem to prefer the swamps, where there is no noise of steamboat to disturb them. All, even the tigers, will flee at the approach of man, but the sportsman who goes tiger-shooting should have complete confidence in his rifle and the steadiness of his nerves, or it may fare ill with him. A large tiger-skin is worth even here 3*l.* or 4*l.* sterling. The water-fowl comprise divers, boobies, cranes, gulls and vultures; I saw some of the last-named feeding on the carcase of a lamb that was floating down stream.

Sometimes through wood-openings, we get a glimpse of Mount Sapocai, the river making so many bends that the peak is one time before us, another right astern, and the sun shifts in like manner till you fancy the mariner's compass has gone quite out of order. At one place, where a saw-mill is working hard by, the turn is so sharp that the steamer has to force its way through the branches of the trees and hug the shore. At last we come upon scattered cottages of neat exterior, and flaxen-haired children run out to look at us, just as the Gothic spire of San Leopoldo comes in view, with an opening vista of the town.

San Leopoldo, founded in 1837, is famous for children and potatoes, in the same way as Kidderminster for carpets, Naples for macaroni, or Sèvres for porcelain. I had heard this ever since my arrival in Rio Grande, and was not surprised, when our vessel got abreast of 'John Muller's tannery,' to see a troop of chubby-faced little boys marching past under the direction of a priest. The moment you land you are struck with the neat German cottages on all sides, and the incredible number of children. But for the tropical luxuriance of the gardens you would fancy yourself in some pleasant country-village of Northern Europe :

the windows have white curtains, between which you see some fair-haired girls or house-wives peep out at the strangers. We proceed to Ernest Koch's hotel in the main-street, which recalls a thousand associations of Fatherland. In front is Her Meitzell's 'bierbrauerei,' next door Julius Fillman's bakery, further on Mr. Huhnfleisch the hat-maker, another shop belonging to a 'buchbinder,' and the large two-story house is the office of the 'New Hamburg and Port Alegre Railway Works.' You hear nothing but German spoken around you. The atmosphere is German, nor can you realise that you are hundreds of miles in the heart of Brazilian forests. Saw-mills wherever you turn, and the hum of industry, giving assurance of peace, progress, and civilisation.

The Germans are a wonderful people : you may call them phlegmatic or what you will, but Nature evidently intended them for colonists *par excellence*. In the United States there are 5,000,000 German settlers (including their children), all thriving farmers, as Mr. Maguire testifies in his work on 'the Irish in America.' They are steady, peaceable, and industrious, and it is not a small merit in a new country that they are eminently domestic and rear up large families in the manner to form good citizens and useful members of society. The German who visits the Port Alegre colonies will find reason to be proud of his countrymen, who form one of the largest and most flourishing communities on this continent. They are also the happiest people on the face of the earth, and you see it depicted on their countenances. Long may they enjoy the Golden Age of their Arcadian simplicity and virtue!

While we were seated at dinner in the hotel, Major Johann Schmidt, commander of the district, came in to pay us a visit accompanied by Mr. Philip Matte, one of the richest colonists; neither of them spoke English, but we got on alternately with German and Portuguese. Mr. Schmidt was born here, but paid a visit to Germany in 1865, and was a spectator of the battle of Skalitz, in Bohemia. He gave me a great deal of information about the colonies, of which more hereafter. A friend of Matte's came in while we were playing billiards; each of these men, I am told, is worth over 20,000*l.* sterling.

It is a lovely moonlight evening, and a number of children are playing on a heap of shavings in the middle of the street, of which presently they make a bonfire, dancing round it with German cries and interjections. My bed-room in the upper story is the neatest thing imaginable, and I lie down to dream of Rasselas and the Happy Valley, the villagers of the Rhine-gau, and the sunniest recollections of a life of travel.

The bell which summons the workmen to their labours, from the neighbouring Gothic steeple, awoke me about sunrise. I sallied forth to have a view of the place, and after a stroll on the river's bank, my attention was called to a refrain sung by children's voices in the church already mentioned. It was a Litany which some 80 boys and girls were singing, under the direction of a Jesuit father, who played the organ, just as we may suppose the Psalms and Litanies to have been sung in the Misiones in the last century, before the expulsion of the Jesuits. The children were all Germans, and their morning prayer echoed in the vaulted aisles of the Gothic building, which was supported by 8 pillars, and lighted by stained glass windows. I remarked that each of the children brought a bunch of flowers and left it in the portico of the church. There is a Protestant church at a short distance, and the foundations have been laid for a Municipal Hall.

The saw-mills were busily working, and the

children going to school with books and bottles of milk, when the town clock struck eight, and the heat was already excessive. I saw strange waggons (12 feet by 3) driven by boys, with loads of timber. Here and there I looked into the shops, which seemed well stocked, until the scorching sun drove me for shelter to the hotel.

As soon as the stately palm-trees began to cast their evening shadows athwart the streets the casements are again thrown open, and the little households seem to breathe the cool air with enjoyment. There is a sudden bustle in our street, as a procession of nine or ten couples, the men wearing white gloves, and the women in gala attire, came out of the Evangelical chapel, having just registered the vows of a bride and bridegroom, who lead the procession, and are the observed of all observers. They are young, honest-looking people, just the *beau-idéal* for colonists, and are followed by old ladies and gentlemen who have probably watched this Paul and Virginia couple from earliest infancy, and now accompany the bride to her new home, wishing her a long career of health and happiness such as has made up their own simple annals. I learn that the harmony between Catholics and Protestants is so great that intermarriages are frequent, and you will often find the good man of the house a Catholic and his helpmate a Protestant, or *vice-versâ*. In numbers the two persuasions are about equally represented, many of the colonists coming from the Rhenish or other Catholic provinces of Germany.

I have learned a good deal about the colonies from Mr. Curtius, editor of 'Der Bote,' and Mr. Philip Leopold Matte, which will form the subject of a separate chapter.

## X.

### INAUGURATION OF THE SAN LEOPOLDO RAILWAY.

Sunday, November 26.

THE little town of San Leopoldo has been all astir since before sunrise, on account of the inauguration, which takes place this afternoon, of the railway works to Porto Alegre. The steamer yesterday brought numbers of people from the capital, who were at some difficulty to find quarters for the night, and sundry merchants and others from Porto Alegre availed themselves of the fine moonlight to make the journey on horseback, a ride of four hours, arriving here in the small hours of daylight and keeping our hostelry in a state of noisy excitement.

By the first streak of dawn you might see the Germans and natives coming in on horseback from the neighbouring hills while the church-bell was ringing for Mass, and the railway people were hurrying about in final preparation for the *fêtes*.

## INAUGURATION OF SAN LEOPOLDO RAILWAY. 95

The President, Bishop, and party, in three steamers, were expected from Porto Alegre by 11 o'clock, the Municipality to receive the distinguished guests, at the water-side, and conduct them to the church and sing a Te Deum. Mr. MacGinity had fixed 7 o'clock A.M. for starting from Porto Alegre, but possibly the low state of the river has caused a delay, as up to the hour I write (2 P.M.) the steamers are not yet in sight.

The church is tastefully decorated, with garlands of evergreens hung between the nave and sanctuary and around the high altar. The villagers are all in holiday costume, numbers of farmers are mounted on steady nags, wearing white ponchos and ponderous silver spurs. All the factories and saw-mills are still, as becomes the Sabbath morning; but the shops and houses are open to receive the crowds of country visitors. Yonder comes a cavalcade of horsemen and women, crossing the river nearly abreast of the church; the water barely reaches to the horses' bellies.

The scene of the day's celebration is the temporary station, about a mile hence, which has been fitted up in admirable style. The building measures 70 feet by 22, and is surmounted at one end by the Brazilian, at the other by the British, flag; all the enclosure of four acres round is decorated with flags of various nations flying from high poles, and in the middle is an awning, where President Mello, after receiving the Bishop's benediction, is to lay the foundation-stone. A stand-house in front, covered in from the tropical sun, is set apart for the ladies who grace the occasion. Just outside the enclosure is a 'ramada' of green boughs, under which the "carne con cuero,' or beef in the hide, is to be roasted for the multitude. The interior of the station is fitted up as a banquet-hall, with four tables for 160 covers, the walls around being hung with bannerets. Over the President's chair are suspended the Brazilian flag and a crown of flowers and bay-leaves; in front is the chair for the Bishop, the rest of the table being arranged for the local authorities. At one end of the hall is a large German flag, at the other the stars and stripes of the great republic.

The silver trowel and spade for the occasion are of elegant workmanship, made at Porto Alegre, the handles being of a dozen kinds of inlaid native wood. The mortar-board is a beautiful piece of cedar, highly polished.

Nothing can be imagined more charming or picturesque than the view on all sides from the station. Northward are ranges of wooded hills, terminating in a line of 'cerros,' the loftiest of which are known as the Dois Irmaos, or Two Brothers; eastward the woods come down so close as to shut out the view, but as we carry our eyes to the south, it rests on the mansion of Spiegelberg, nestling in a plantation which extends to the summit of the hill behind; to the west we descry the Gothic spire of San Leopoldo over-topping the orange-trees of the suburbs, among which also peeps out Mr. MacGinity's chacra, or country-house. The town is not visible through the luxuriant foliage, though barely 700 yards distant.

3 P.M.

The squire of Spiegelberg gives a grand ball this evening, besides two others in San Leopoldo. The brass band of the town is playing lively airs through the streets, and the policemen are letting off rockets; but the President is not yet come.

The steamers have just arrived, and the President, Bishop, and party are gone to sing Te Deum in the church. The heat is so excessive that the inauguration is put off till six o'clock.

At the appointed hour the scene of festivity is crowded with three thousand persons, chiefly Germans. Major Schmidt has the police force of

H

the town (six men), guarding the triumphal arch. The military band from Port Alegre announces the approach of the President and Bishop, who are received at the entrance by Messrs. MacGinity, Bevan Smith, Cleary, Sawer, Turner, &c., and conducted to the place where the stone is to be laid. The President wears the uniform of Senator of the Empire with the Star of the order of the Rose; the Bishop has a purple soutanne under a lace rochette, and is accompanied by a Jesuit priest and some others. The stone is a ponderous slab of red sandstone. The Bishop gives the signal to uncover and pronounces the usual prayers on such occasions, lasting about ten minutes, after which the police let off rockets, the band strikes up the Brazilian hymn, and the people cheer. His Excellency President Mello next delivered a very appropriate and eloquent speech, expatiating on the benefits which the enterprise was destined to produce, wishing every success to those Englishmen under whose intelligent direction it is to be carried out, and promising his steadiest co-operation towards prolonging the line to the Argentine frontier.

Mr. King, a clever photographer, takes a view of the ceremonial at the moment when Messrs. MacGinity and Bevan Smith are depositing a box in the hollow of the foundation-stone containing coins, local newspapers, and such like. Then the laying of the stone is gone through, the engineers presenting the silver trowel to the President of the Province, and the spade to the municipal guild of San Leopoldo, the inscription on the latter being—'This spade was used by Pres. Mello to turn the first sod at San Leopoldo, of the New Hamburg Railway, in presence of John MacGinity, concessionaire; H. Bleary, engineer; Bevan Smith, contractor; and an assembled multitude, this 26th day of November, 1871.'

We now proceed to the banquet-hall, where the tables were sumptuously spread, and I chanced to be placed near the President and Bishop. During the dinner the President assured me that General Mitre was highly respected in Brazil, as well as our actual chief magistrate, President Sarmiento.

The first toast was given by Mr. MacGinity— 'The Government of President Mello, under whose administration every enterprise for the advancement of Rio Grande found the most cordial support.' (Cheers.)

This was warmly received with three times three, the band playing a Portuguese melody.

Mr. Thompson, an Anglo-Brazilian, in proposing the next toast said—'On an occasion like the present we must not forget the claims of the Legislature of Rio Grande, which came forward with a liberal subsidy in the form of a guarantee on the capital, to stimulate the introduction of railways into this Province. It was a purpose which enlisted all their sympathies and patriotism, for the legislators felt that the locomotive was the great civiliser of new countries, the conqueror of modern times, uniting peoples and communities, founding societies where before was desert, and therefore more glorious than the destroying cannon which men are too apt to regard with honour. He trusted all present would unite with him in toasting the Legislature of the Province.'

Dr. Guzman, Secretary of State, said—'There is yet a meed of honour due to one now absent, I mean ex-President Sartore, who contracted for this great work, and whose health I give you.' (Cheers.)

Dr. Teofilo Ribeyro, Secretary of Government, rose and said—'Ladies and gentlemen, I look on this happy festivity as the inauguration of a new era of peace and labour still more prolific than any we have yet seen in Rio Grande. The whistle of the engine will awaken the echoes of our virgin woods, and at the same time our telegraph system, already connecting this Province with Rio Janeyro, is now pushing forward rapidly towards the countries of the River Plate; while the growth of our German colonies is marvellous and our immigration spontaneous. May Divine Providence continue His blessings to this favoured land!'

The last speaker having made allusion to the River Plate, of which I was the only representative present, I felt bound to say a few words. I assured the Rio Grandenses that their neighbours of La Plata would feel most happy to learn of their progress in enterprises like the present, for which I offered them the warmest congratulation, adding that I hoped this railway would be pushed on, as proposed, to the frontier of the Argentine Republic, to unite neighbouring peoples in the lasting bonds of international traffic.

The next toast was given by Dr. Ferraz, 'To the foreigners who came among us to develope the resources of the country, and make Rio Grande a free, prosperous, and enlightened State.'

Some one next proposed the Fourth Estate, coupling with it the names of Guttenberg and the Rio Grande Editors.

President Mello rose to thank Mr. MacGinity in the first place for having proposed his health, and then begged the company to join him in a toast to the Paranhos Cabinet, for having carried out two of the greatest measures that could fall to the lot of any statesman, the Judicial Reform and the Abolition of Slavery; the latter by far the greater, since it consecrated the precepts of the Gospel which regarded all men as entitled to equal rights. This great measure, he repeated, would immortalise the name of Viscount Rio Branco. The toast was drunk, all standing, with three times three.

Mr. MacGinity, in a very graceful manner, proposed the Municipality of San Leopoldo, expatiating on their civic visitors, and afterwards gave the health of Mr. Bevan Smith, of the firm of Watson Smith, contractors for the line (cheers).

Mr. Guzman proposed the Engineers, and especially Mr. Cleary. The latter replied in a finished Portuguese speech, and proposed 'The New Hamburg Railway Company.'

Mr. Bevan Smith proposed 'The Ladies, who cheer our rugged road of life, and help to keep us in the track of honour and duty.' (Enthusiastic cheers.)

President Mello, in conclusion, gave the health of His Majesty the Emperor and the Imperial family. 'Every Brazilian had reason to be proud of Dom Pedro, the first citizen of his country and a model ruler. In his present journey through Europe, he has been everywhere received as a liberal monarch, sound statesman, and advanced scholar, while he is still better known in Brazil as a man of domestic virtues and polished taste, an encourager of industrial enterprise, a friend to the poor, and a true patriot. May he long be spared to pilot the destinies of the vast empire over which he rules.'

The band struck up the Brazilian hymn, and the feast concluded at 8 P.M.

Monday, 11 A.M.

The President having invited Mr. Smith to remain till this afternoon and accompany him to Port Alegre, I am enabled to add a postscript. Whilst I write, the band is playing a march to the riverside, where His Excellency lays the foundation-stone of the bridge to be placed for public traffic over the Rio dos Linos. Afterwards the school-children have some amateur theatricals in reference to the Railway Inauguration, at which President Mello and the Bishop will assist. The balls last night were brilliant and well attended. Some of the principal townsfolk are sending in mineralogical curiosities and other little souvenirs to Mr. Bevan Smith to take with him to England. All the neighbours evince the liveliest interest in the railway. The engineers accompany Mr. Smith to Port Alegre, and I start in the morning for three days' ride through the woods to the great waterfall in the Tea-forest.

## XI.

## A RIDE THROUGH THE COLONIES.

THE traveller who would visit each and all of the German settlements in the district of Port Alegre must devote at least a month to the task; but as the whole forty-four are very similar in character, it will be enough to make a tour of four or five days from San Leopoldo through the Baumschneitz valley, New Hamburg, Acht-und-Vierzig, Tea-forest, Caffee-Schneitz, and intermediate 'picadas,' under the guidance of a good 'vaqueano,' to form an accurate idea of the colonies. Without a personal visit of this kind it is difficult to realise the nature and importance of these settlements. Imagine to yourself, reader, a country nearly as large as Belgium or Holland cut out of these Brazilian forests, where the inhabitants are exclusively German, and speak no other language; where chapels and schools meet you at every opening in the wood; where the mountain-sides have been in many cases cleared to make room for corn-fields; where women travel alone through the forests in perfect security; where agricultural and manufacturing industry flourish undisturbed; where crime is unknown and public instruction almost on a level with that of Prussia; in a word, where individual happiness and the welfare of the commonwealth go hand-in-hand, surrounded by the rich, tropical vegetation of Brazil, and favoured by the great advantages of a healthy climate, and the blessings of peace, order, and good government.

Among the townsfolk of San Leopoldo, few are more obliging than Herr Philip Matté, and through his agency I found an excellent guide, one Cornelius, who also provided horses for the journey. At 6 A.M., on November 28, we started, under the auspices of a cloudy morning, and crossed the Rio dos Sinos near where the proposed bridge is to be built, the water being above the horses' bellies; in wet seasons it is impassable. On the opposite bank are some neat cottages, and a large house belonging to one Schmidt. Emerging from the town, we find an open country of some extent, with a half-moon of hills in front, and on the left a series of undulating woods. Yonder is a stone cross in memory of Johann Stievenbach, who was dragged with a lasso from San Leopoldo, and murdered on this spot by one of the contending factions in the civil war of the Farapos.

My guide tells me of several deeds of atrocity in that dreadful time. The Germans had hoped to be left undisturbed in their little farms, but first the rebels, and then the government troops, dragged them away from their homes and families, impressing them for the war. In this manner it often happened that father and son were ranged on opposite sides. The colonists were ruined, and had no means of escaping from the country, which was a scene of bloodshed and desolation for more than ten years, till the pacification of 1845 put a stop to these horrors, and allowed the colonists to pursue peaceful pursuits.

Ascending the slope of Lomba Grande, we meet some waggons bound for San Leopoldo, with a blue-eyed *fraulein* sitting on the sacks of Indian corn; and now we get in view of Hamburger Berg, crowned with a little chapel, behind which we soon discern the roof-tops of New Hamburg. This picturesque village covers the hill-side, and down in the valley my guide points out the house of the richest colonist, a mixture of Swiss cottage and English farm-house. The village inn is neat and comfortable; in the parlour there is a picture of Shakespeare's Seven Ages of Man. Passing the Protestant chapel, and a fine house belonging to an apothecary named Kastrup, we emerge from New Hamburg, the terminus of the first section of the Port Alegre railroad, and enter at once into a woody and mountainous country.

We are now in the Schwabe-Schneitz, so called from the Swabians who made the first clearing here. At intervals we come upon water-mills, rustic school-houses, troops of mules carrying grain to San Leopoldo, and at every wood-opening we see the colonists, men and women, busy at their daily labours in the field. The usual hours for work are from six to eleven in the morning, and two to seven in the afternoon, thus avoiding the intense heat of mid-day.

At some of the steepest passes the colonists have made a paved road, practicable either for mules or the peculiar little cart of the country. From one of these points we have a splendid view of the surrounding country, generally known as Bom Jardin, with the twin peaks of Dos Irmaos, and in the distance New Hamburg and San Leopoldo.

The forest scenery varies at every turn, in weird vistas of grandeur and solitude. Wild orange and fig trees appear at times among the thick woods of valuable timber of a dozen different kinds, and brushwood and creepers are so closely intertwined that it would be difficult to force your way through. We begin to descend, and a view opens upon us of the Baumschneitz Valley. As we enter the village a bridal procession sallies forth from the Catholic chapel, just such a building as you see on the Rhine, with a wooden belfry: the bride is young and fair, and the whole cavalcade start off to accompany the happy pair to their new home in the woods.

At Baumschneitz there is a good inn, kept by Carl Merkel. Travellers going to the Tea-forest and Waterfall generally finish the first day's journey here, as the route over the mountains is very fatiguing. Nevertheless, as the day was cloudy, I resolved to make a double day's journey and push on for the Waterfall.

The main street of Baumschneitz is lined with orange trees. The houses are models of neatness. At the farther end we find the Protestant chapel and minister's house; then the houses are more scattered and less tasteful. The better kind are of bricks, with a wooden half-story under the sloping roof. Many, however, are of mud and canes, or made in a species of framework, with the large cross-beams conspicuous, as in most of the hamlets of Germany. Beneath the cottage, however humble, is a basement used for storing implements, which keeps the habitations very dry. No bars or bolts are visible, and the windows are often without glass.

Crossing Millersberg, we see the mountains around us cultivated to their summits, and ahead of us, perched like an eagle's eyrie, is Woolff's Nest, a well-known wayside inn. Away to the left the hills recede till lost in an outline of woods in the direction of Caffee-schneitz. Not far from thence it is proposed to establish an Irish colony, and Mr. MacGinity, concessionaire of the railway and other enterprises, intends to give settlers free land grants of 100 acres. The soil is excellent, and peculiarly favourable, it being so near the railway now in construction.

Ascending Fritzberg the road becomes little better than a dry river-bed. Wood-pigeons abound here. At last, after arduous toiling up hill, we reach Woolff's Nest. What a lovely panorama! In the foreground the Dos Irmaos and Sapocai, at our feet the peaceful valley of Baumschneitz, and on all sides a diversified picture of woods, plains, farm-houses, and undulating hills, till the blue line of the horizon is broken on the far right by the white buildings of Port Alegre, fifty miles distant as the crow flies.

Herr Woolff and his wife are hospitable people, and do a thriving business, their house being a general store of dry goods, groceries, &c., and on Sunday evenings the neighbours meet here to dance. The ball-room measures 40 by 36 feet, with a corner set apart for the orchestra. Everything about the place bespeaks neatness. The woods close it in on either side, while the mountain rises up precipitously behind. A steep ascent conducts us to the summit, where a cross-road occurs, and now we are on the top of a ridge commanding a delightful view, whichever way we turn. The road to the right leads into the Tea-forest. Before many minutes we seem plunged in the heart of dense woods, which create a feeling of silence and solemnity, as if you were beneath the vaulted roof of some old Gothic cathedral. We journey on for nearly an hour in this manner, and suddenly come upon a cavalcade of a dozen persons. It is the Grafin von Eberstein, a German baroness of sixty summers, who is at present making a tour of the world à la Ida Pfeiffer, and whose arrival last week at San Leopoldo caused some sensation. She is attended by an ugly maid-servant, a muscular courier, three or four of the colonists, a guide, the parson of Baumschneitz, and some others. She rides a strong cob, seated in a kind of arm-chair, and has made a difficult journey to and from the Waterfall, apparently without fatigue. We are again in the depths of the forest. What splendid ferns! What stately trees, all interlaced with creepers and parasites!

Emerging from the forest we saw the sun descending behind the woods of the Rosen Thal, when our road diverged to the right and left at a little chapel, near which there was no house for us to ask which way we should follow. Beside the chapel was a tasteful churchyard, or 'God's acre,' as the Germans call it, with sundry stone crosses and flower-beds. My guide resolved on taking the lower road, to the left, with some uncertainty as to whether we should have to pass the night in the woods. But before darkness set in we came to a turn in the mountain which disclosed a group of cottages. Passing a small cloth-mill and another chapel, we began to ascend another range of hills, for my guide now remembered the locality, and said we should have to pass the night at the shanty of Herr Rost, near the Waterfall. At times the path was so precipitous and full of loose stones that we had to alight and lead our horses. The full summer moon was sailing on her course as we reached Herr Rost's, where we found a frugal supper and clean beds of Indian corn straw, after a long day's ride of thirteen hours.

## XII.

### *FROM THE WATERFALL TO THE DEVIL'S GLEN.*

It was my purpose to see the first rays of the sun fall on the Caté cascade, and some time before sunrise we were making our way through Herr Rost's wood-clearing, where patches of beans and flax alternated with felled timber. The descent into the ravine is no longer so dangerous as formerly, but you must beware of the loose stones.

The first view of the waterfall disappoints you, the quantity of water being insignificant; its height by degrees impresses you, for it is 375 feet over a sheer precipice, the woods on either side coming down to the brink, while the waterfall like a silver ribbon descends to the valley; there is no visible outlet for the water, which is caught in a pool that has never been sounded, and the neighbours have a tradition of a man who fell in and was never seen to rise, his body having been probably carried away by some subterranean current. At the falls of the Anio, in Tivoli, there is a similar pool, called Neptune's Grotto, with a subterranean outlet.

A thin vapour rises from the cascade, which assumes many colours as the sunbeams fall on it. An Englishman took a photograph of this waterfall some time ago, and to give an idea of its height, he caused twenty men to stand in a line with their hands joined, over the precipice. The noise of the fall is trifling, but in winter the volume of water is much greater, and often carries down cattle with it.

From the waterfall my route lay again through the Tea-forest to Baumschneitz, from which I intended making a *détour* by the Devil's Glen and Acht-und-Vierzig. In the middle of the forest we met two women on horseback; as a rule the women in these colonies ride like men, for the same reason as in the mountainous parts of Italy, since sidesaddles would be very insecure. The only birds you hear in these forests are the Tanzen-Vögel or Dancing-birds, the 'blacksmith,' 'carpenter,' &c. The dancing-birds are blue with red tops: five of them perch in a line on the branch of a tree, the leader sings, and the others hop backwards and forwards like soldiers on drill. The blacksmith is a white bird with black top: the noise he makes seems at a distance like a hammer striking on an anvil. At rare intervals you see a monkey.

Descending from Woolff's to the valley we meet numbers of children coming from school, two on each horse, boys and girls, making their way through the woods homewards. We arrive at Carl Merkel's inn at Baumschneitz in time for dinner, and halt here for the night. The landlord was formerly a soldier of Rosas in Buenos Ayres, some twenty years ago, and came hither just before the campaign of Caseros which overthrew that ruler.

About sunset I took a stroll through the quiet village, where the housewives were throwing open their doors and windows, the children were playing under the orange-trees, some fowlers were coming home from the forest with bags full of game, and a group of people was gathered at the smithy watching the operation of shoeing a restive horse. I turned into the graveyard of the Catholic chapel and read the inscriptions which tell the simple annals of the first settlers, some born by the North Sea sands, some by the foaming Danube, some in the Black Forest, some by the sunny Rhine; the oldest date I could find was 1837, showing that this colony must have been ten years after San Leopoldo. An avenue from the graveyard leads to the Jesuit glebe hard by, where half-a-dozen fathers reside belonging to the surrounding settlements. There is neither doctor nor apothecary in the village, no prison or police; the inhabitants are simple in their habits, marry young, have large families, and are usually long-lived. During the Paraguayan war the place had to furnish a contingent of twenty-six men, of whom only five returned. It is pleasant, as the shades of night descend, to watch the wood-cutters' fires, or the lights from the little homesteads on the mountain sides. The fire-flies flit about, and the village is settling down to repose; the smithy is shut, and the moon rises, pouring her silvery light upon wood and mountain. It is worthy of note that the fire-flies in the River Plate carry the lantern in their tails, but here it is on their heads, and the light is clearer.

An hour before sunrise I was again on the road, by moonlight, leaving the valley of Baumschneitz behind. At a short distance the path plunged into a dense forest, and before we emerged from it we could see the first beams of morning shining on the tree-tops. The magnificent woodland scenery fully compensates for the difficulties of the path: every now and then we have to bend low or sideways to avoid the species of wild vines that hang like ropes from the lofty branches, forming the most fantastic network from tree to tree. After a couple of hours' riding, in which we met nobody, a forest-opening occurred, and we saw a field of magnificent palms, passing which we were again in the woods, until the crowing of a cock announced that we were near some human habitation, and presently we found ourselves at a comfortable farm-house, the owner of which, in reply to my guide's questions, pointed over a thickly-wooded ridge towards Acht-und-Vierzig, adding that the way was almost impracticable. He sent his little girl to open for us the gate of the fence which separated his holding from the glen. The descent at once began to be steep, the path stony and difficult, and before a quarter of an hour I almost repented not having taken the farmer's advice and turned back. At one place it was like descending a rickety stone staircase, as we led our horses gently by the head, and even so the poor beasts stumbled so often that at times I feared they should fall on us. At last we reached the foot, where a valley spread out ahead of us, the steep sides being clad with thickest timber, and a small river running in the middle of the low ground, which we skirted. A peculiar noise called my attention, and I was puzzled to think what it might be, until my guide said it was caused by apes holding a morning confabulation; the din being caused by the animals striking their mouths with their paws.

The colonists see little of the apes, which generally make their haunts in secluded woods, near fresh water, and dislike the proximity of human beings. Crossing the stream we came to a large cavern or hollow of the mountain, that leans over the path as if ready to overwhelm the traveller. On the top of the cliff are farm-houses invisible to us, and yonder we see some little boys with satchels making their way afoot to the school of Acht-und-Vierzig: the woods are still thick, and the scenery charming at each fresh vista. Here we come upon a fine orange-grove near the ruins of a house; a woman is driving a cow before her. As the valley again opens we see in the distance, overtopping the woods, the turret of the village chapel, which crowns the hill-side. The river running through the valley is crossed by a massive stone bridge, 400 yards long and 30 feet high, which cost over 30,000*l*. Formerly numbers of colonists and others perished in trying to cross here in rainy seasons, and whether from this circumstance or from the gloomy scenery around, the place is called the Devil's Glen.

A steep ascent leads from the bridge to the village on the hill. The principal trader of the place is Herr Kossel; a good shop is also kept by Frau Blauet: the inn is clean and comfortable, and as usual there is a large ball-room, 40 feet square, with a gallery for the musicians: here the villagers have their monthly balls. The chapel is built in the same style as all the rest in the colonies, but it is to be noted that the Protestant chapels have no turret or belfry. The graveyard has but few tombstones, and in a meadow hard-by we see a Jesuit reading his breviary.

Riding through the village we attract the notice of the inhabitants, and as we pass the school the children seem well-ordered at their tasks. As we ascend Bergsmerberg, a long and gentle acclivity, we observe gardens, cottages, and a Protestant chapel, in a very diversified landscape. Half-an-hour farther finds us in dense woods, where we meet two ladies unaccompanied and riding side-saddle. As the woods open we come out on a cloth-mill built over a little stream, with a jolly-looking miller and comfortable residence. A couple of miles farther we come to a wayside shop kept by a smart-looking woman, who kindly gave us permission to rest, for the sun was now hot. She had neither meat nor eggs, but sent out her little boy to dig some potatoes for us (these people are great vegetarians), and offered to borrow some hay from a neighbour for our horses. As we were, however, very hungry, having had nothing all day but a cup of coffee at Acht-und-Vierzig, we resolved to push on to San Leopoldo for dinner. Wild, bare mountain scenery succeeded, affording us a fine view of the country: to the left we are leaving behind us the Dos Irmaos, and to the right lies the Caffee-schneitz, while ahead of us is the Farapoi Wood, famous for guerilla combats in the civil war. Below the wood is a pleasant valley, and yonder snug farm-house belongs to Carl Wilk. A few paces from our path we are startled to observe the body of a man: as we proceed to dismount, Cornelius remarks to me that he must have died of a fit or exposure to the sun. The body was not quite stiff, but to all appearance dead, until Cornelius exclaimed, 'It is warm, he cannot be dead;' and turning up the face, we saw it was a poor old negro slave, who presently opened his eyes. The smell of cashaso was intolerable, for the old fellow had been on a drunken spree, having probably obtained a holiday from his master, Herr Wilk. Had he remained there a few hours longer the sun must have killed him. We meet several waggons returning to the hills, most of them with oil casks, having left their produce at San Leopoldo, the church of which is now distinctly visible. Traversing some miles of low, sandy ground, from which the glare of the sun is most distressing, we reach the Rio dos Sinos and wade it at a depth of five feet, arriving at Koch's comfortable hotel in time for dinner.

## XIII.

### THE GERMAN COLONIES: THEIR ORIGIN, GROWTH, AND PRESENT CONDITION.

THE first colony was that of San Leopoldo, established by the present Emperor's father, Dom Pedro I., in the fertile lands of the old Féitoria Real de Canhamo (Royal flax factory), still called Féitoria Velha, on the banks of the Sinos river, now forty-seven years ago. The first batch of settlers, comprising 26 families and 17 unmarried persons, arrived on June 25, 1825, to the number of 126 souls, and were followed some months later by 157 families numbering 909 persons. In the four subsequent years the arrivals reached 3,701; but the civil wars which ensued put a stop to immigration until the renewal of peace in 1844, the number of arrivals in 1846 amounting to 1,515. A census taken in 1854 showed the colonists to number 11,172 souls, including 3,680 children born in the country, occupying 2,083 houses. The increase by births over deaths was amazing, and the number of colonists was also increased by the disbanded battalions of German chasseurs and grenadiers after the war, who received, like the soldiers of Augustus, free land-grants, that they might turn their swords into reaping-hooks, and each man sit down under the shadow of his own fig-tree. In 1866 the Inspector of Colonies reported the number of Germans (including children born in the country) at 25,000 in the single district of San Leopoldo, and their farm-lots ranged in value from 10 to 28 contos (say 1,000*l.* to 2,800*l.* sterling).

When we bear in mind that the colony at the very outset had to encounter a civil war which lasted nearly twenty years, and in which the colonists themselves were forced to take part on opposing sides, it is simply marvellous what progress San Leopoldo has made, now 'the richest, most productive, and most populous district in the Province of Rio Grande.'

The first settlers received free-grants each of 130 acres uncleared land, besides farming-implements, seeds, and a subsidy for their support: this subsidy consisted of a pataca (about a shilling) ahead per day for the first year, and half a pataca the second. The total number of immigrants alive in the colony in 1854 was 7,492, the rest having either died naturally or perished in the wars, at the conclusion of which in 1846 San Leopoldo was found to be only a heap of ruins.

Peace, however, no sooner smiled upon the country than the growth of this colony was prodigious, and it has gone on increasing since the formation of the municipality in 1854. Now every year hundreds of young men leave San Leopoldo for the districts of Triumfo, San Jeronimo, Taquary, Bocca-do-Monte, forming new settlements which radiate in all directions, clearing away the virgin forests and extending the fruits of industry far and wide.

In 1854 the exports of San Leopoldo represented 91,200*l.* sterling; in 1867 they were estimated at nine times that amount. In 1854 the commerce maintained 282 flat-boats; now it requires steam-boats and railways. In 1854 the lands of the colonists were valued at 600,000*l.* sterling, but now they represent ten times that figure. In 1854 the manufactures of San Leopoldo comprised 67,000 sets of harness and 3,300*l.* worth of tanned hides. At present it would be impossible to enumerate the saw-mills, oil-presses, breweries, tanyards, distilleries, sugar-presses, and manufactories of hats, firearms, iron-work, &c. established at San Leopoldo, Hamburgerberg, Féitoria, Hortensio, and the country round. All the saddlery for the army, farmers, &c., is made here, as well as the lances, spurs, and accoutrements; and tanned hides are sent to all parts of the empire, while San Leopoldo also supplies Port Alegre with butter, eggs, fowls, pork, &c. The official report estimates the produce of San Leopoldo alone at 10,000 contos or one million sterling per annum.

Of late years the colonists have begun to cultivate vines, and now the yield is over a thousand pipes of wine yearly. They are also giving some attention to bees, for the production of honey and wax; and as flax and cotton are easily cultivated, there is an increasing home manufacture of these staples with the rudest and simplest appliances. At an exhibition of arts, products, and manufactures for the Province of Rio Grande, in 1866, more than three-fourths of the prizes fell to German colonists.

Meantime it is thought that the colonies would have made even greater progress if more care had been given to their first establishment. Major Schaeffer, who engaged the first colonists in Germany on the part of the Brazilian Government, did not select the most suitable persons, such as small peasant farmers, but took them all as they came, and to the present day we find among the old colonists a mixture of shoemakers, coopers, saddlers, charcoal-burners, &c., who in the beginning felt so little disposition for agriculture that when some of them were settled down here they sold their grants for a bottle of brandy. Then again the authorities had not properly measured and marked out the ground, which was considered a trifling matter; but when land subsequently became of value, the number of disputed titles was so confusing that a special commission was at last sent by Government to restore order and confirm rights, but not before some of the most industrious colonists had thrown up their farms in disgust and removed to the new German colonies that were being formed on the River Plate.

The municipal returns of San Leopoldo show that the exports of the district have almost trebled in sixteen years. The amount of duties levied in 1854 was about 800*l.*, and in 1870 was 2,200*l.* sterling. The municipal revenue of San Leopoldo is said to exceed that of Rio Grande city, and the imperial blue-books of the Rio

Janeyro speak of San Leopoldo as the most flourishing agricultural department in Brazil. The exports for the year ending June 30, 1870, were as follow:—

| | | |
|---|---|---:|
| Beans, | sacks | 34,852 |
| Maize | ,, | 42,783 |
| Potatoes | ,, | 5,972 |
| Starch | ,, | 177 |
| Bacon, | lbs. | 220,000 |
| Lard | ,, | 460,000 |
| Tobacco | ,, | 105,000 |
| Bark | ,, | 2,400 |
| Yerba-mate, | ,, | 8,500 |
| Hair | ,, | 110,000 |
| Saddles | | 3,529 |
| Lombillas | | 3,651 |
| Caronos | | 3,918 |
| Sandals, pairs | | 71,630 |
| Slippers | ,, | 30,371 |
| Cowhides | | 11,159 |
| Swine, heads | | 172 |
| Aguardiente, pipes | | 120 |
| Firewood, measures | | 5,426 |
| Lumber, value | | £2,356 |

Add to this such important items as butter, eggs, poultry, &c., which are free of duties and not included in the above. To the general reader, who may be anxious to know what Lombillas and Caronos are, we can only say that they are parts of harness or saddlery which the colonists make especially for the army and exportation to the northern provinces.

# THE GERMAN COLONIES: THEIR ORIGIN. 129

The colonies which have grown out of San Leopoldo, or been subsequently established in Rio Grande, are now 43 in number, mostly radiating around the first settlement and promising to rival it in prosperity: they are—

| | |
|---|---|
| Lomba Grande | Larangeiras |
| New Hamburg | Maratá |
| Costa da Serra | Bocca do Monte |
| Baumschneitz | Bom Jardin |
| Dos Irmaos | Novo Petropolis |
| Campo Bom | Germania |
| Caffee-schneitz | Silva |
| Achtundviersig-schneitz | El Rey |
| Hortense-schneitz | Santa Cruz |
| Picada Feliz | Mont Alverne |
| Picada Voluntaria | Soledade |
| Picada Solitaria | Sant Angelo |
| Picada Demanda | Cima da Serra |
| Sommer-schneitz | Sinimbu |
| Capibary-schneitz | Camaquam |
| Montravel | San Lorenzo |
| Mundo Novo | Estrella |
| Conventos | Tres Forquilhas |
| Morro dos Bois | San Pedro |
| Costa Cahy | Teutonia |
| Padre Eterno | Paricy. |

Two of the above, namely Tres Forquilhas and San Pedro, are nearly as old as San Leopoldo, having been founded in 1826, but have not been so prosperous. The position chosen for them was remote and unsuitable, on the margin of Lake

K

Itapebe, separated by 120 miles of forest from San Leopoldo, and near the projected seaport of Torres between Sta Catalina and Rio Grande: the twin colonies were founded in this way. Ninety families were selected, and 53 of these (Protestants) were located at Tres Forquilhas, the remaining 37 (Catholics) being placed on a site called San Pedro de Alcantara, nearer Torres. The proposed harbour of refuge was never constructed (although official surveys have again been made recently), and the two colonies were cut off from all communication till 1849, when a road was made from the valley of Tres Forquilhas to Cima da Serra, where the river from which the colony takes its name has its head-waters. A little after the foundation of Tres Forquilhas many of the colonists became very much disgusted, and 17 families returned to San Leopoldo, the other 36 remaining to contend with the difficulties of their situation. For a quarter of a century they had neither roads nor communication with the rest of the province: their progress was, therefore, slow, but not the less certain. Latest returns show its population to have quadrupled, being 80 families or 700 souls, with 75 comfortable houses, a Protestant chapel and pastor, 2 schools (one paid by the State), 4 shops, 8 tanyards, 3 carpenters, 5 shoemakers, 3 boat-builders, &c.; besides ten flour-mills, 8 distilleries, and 28 'atafonas' for grinding mandioca. The colony is at present in a highly flourishing condition, the lands being well cultivated and yielding large quantities of sugar-cane, mandioca, and rice for exportation, not to speak of maize, beans, and potatoes for home consumption. Coffee is also found to thrive here, as well as the cotton plant. The colonists at the same time occupy themselves in handicrafts (as in each and all of these German colonies), and at every house you find a sugar-mill or distillery for aguardiente, or some of the family busy in making 'rapaduras,' of which they export 250,000 yearly. The other annual products include 3,000 bushels of mandioca, and about 500*l*. worth of minor articles, such as pork, cotton, &c.

San Pedro or Torres has a similar history to Tres Forquilhas, and since the 'renaissance' of 1849 has made the same remarkable progress, the latest returns showing 511 souls (in 86 families), of which there were 264 males and 247 females. The school is attended by 50 children. The colony is situated 12 miles from Torres Point, and counts 29 sugar-mills or distilleries, 31 'atafonas' for mandioca, 1 beer-brewery, 1 tanyard, 2 oil-mills, 1 saddlery, 6 shops, 5 blacksmiths, 3 shoemakers, 3 carpenters, and a doctor. The annual produce of the colony includes 382 pipes aguardiente, 250 cwt. of sugar, 4,850 sacks mandioca, 100 sacks polvillo, 500 sacks maize, 200 sacks beans, 250 sacks rice, 150 sacks potatoes, 40,000 tiles, 60,000 bricks, 190 sets harness, 1,000 lbs. glue, &c.

There are no tables extant of the amount of money laid out by the Imperial Government on the three colonies of San Leopoldo, Tres Forquilhas, and Torres, the settlers of which received their lands free, besides an absolute gift in the way of farming implements, provisions, &c. It is, however, admitted that any such outlay has been repaid a hundredfold in the income and duties from the single district of San Leopoldo. If the proposed railway from Port Alegre to Torres be carried out, the other two colonies will soon be equally prosperous.

The sons of the colonists of San Leopoldo soon spread themselves and formed the following new settlements, at short distances from San Leopoldo:—

| | | | |
|---|---|---|---|
| Capibary-schneitz | 14 farms, | distance | 12 miles |
| Sommer-schneitz | 63 ,, | ,, | 20 ,, |
| Picada Demanda | 45 ,, | ,, | 20 ,, |

| | | | | |
|---|---|---|---|---|
| Picada Solitaria . . | 40 farms, | distance | 30 | miles |
| Picada Voluntaria . | 30 ,, | ,, | 30 | ,, |
| Morro dos Bois . . | 50 ,, | ,, | 12 | ,, |
| Costa Cahy . . . . | 18 ,, | ,, | 25 | ,, |
| Padre Eterno . . . | 200 ,, | ,, | 12 | ,, |
| Larangeiras . . . | 100 ,, | ,, | 20 | ,, |
| Santa Maria or Bocca do Monte . . . } | 100 ,, | ,, | 200 | ,, |

But even before these there were Tomba Grande, New Hamburg, Costa da Serra, Bom Jardin, Dos Irmaos, Baumschneitz, Campo Bom, Achtundviersig, Caffee-schneitz, Picada Hortense, Cuatro Colonias, and Picada Feliz: these twelve settlements are very prosperous and count no fewer than 23 churches and 46 schools, the latter attended by 1,045 boys and 697 girls: 31 of these schools are maintained by the colonists, and 15 by the State.

In 1849, after the conclusion of the civil war, the Provincial Government of Rio Grande, under President Andreas, endeavoured to revive the above system of German colonisation, marking out free land-grants at Santa Cruz, 100 miles from Port Alegre, and 20 from the town of Rio Pardo, on an affluent of the River Jacuhy. The lands were fertile, the site excellent, and the colony has been a brilliant success. The first batch of settlers, thirteen in number, arrived in December 1849, two others in the ensuing year, and the beginning of 1851 counted 145 souls in the colony, including thirty colonists' sons from San Leopoldo. The same year a contract was made by Vice-President Bello with Peter Klendgen to bring out 2,000 Germans in two years, the latter proceeding to Germany and offering land-grants, with the sole obligation of repaying advance for implements and supplies: he could not fulfil his contract—the people that were willing to come not being able to pay their passage. At last, in November 1854, a new colonisation-law was passed which gave an immense impetus to the rising settlements: the Government of Rio Grande advanced 5$l$. sterling per head for the passage of immigrants, and sold them the land at reasonable prices, payable in five yearly instalments, along with the above 5$l$. At the close of 1854 the colony only counted 891 inhabitants, occupying 304 land-grants, the Government having expended over 9,000$l$. in their assistance; each successive year saw the colony progress rapidly, and latest returns show 5,083 settlers, occupying an area of 240,000 acres. They have 3 Catholic and 4 Protestant chapels, 13 schools (including 3 supported by the State), 11 flour-mills, 2 'atafonas,' 11 sugar-mills, 5 oil-presses, 5 tanyards, 1 soap-factory, 1 yerba-factory, 1 rope-walk, 1 chandlery, 2 cartwrights, 11 blacksmiths, 26 tailors, 47 shoemakers, 3 saddlers, 51 carpenters, 41 stonecutters, 26 shopkeepers. The total population is 4,794, of whom 2,403 are Catholics and 2,394 Protestants: they compose 988 families, with 1,584 children. Most of the colonists are in the prime of life, only 180 being over fifty years. The exports of the colony are estimated at 18,000$l.$ sterling, and the imports at 16,500$l.$ Their annual crop is valued at 25,000$l.$, of which one-third stands for tobacco, one-fourth maize, and the rest beans, potatoes, barley, wine, sugar-cane, rice, flax, &c., including 5,000 pounds of cotton, and an equal quantity of honey.

Rincon del Rey was founded about the same time as Santa Cruz (1850), not by the State, but by Dr. Israel Barcellos, who induced a number of German families, chiefly from San Leopoldo, to settle on his lands near the town of Rio Pardo, which they supply with milk, butter, eggs, honey, vegetables, &c.: this colony is flourishing.

Mundo Novo was also founded in 1850, by a gentleman named Tristan Monteiro, on lands which he bought a few years before on the Arroyo Santa Maria, 30 miles north-east of San Leopoldo.

He sold the farm-lots at 30*l.* each, and soon found colonists, not only from San Leopoldo, but also from Germany, the situation being well chosen, on the high-road to Cima da Serra. Its progress has been wonderful: in 1853 it had only 4 shops, and now its import trade represents 45,000*l.* per annum, while its exports of maize, tobacco, wine, sugar-cane, beans, brandy, &c., are still more valuable. There are 2 churches; St. Mary's (Protestant) and St. Rose (Catholic), besides 12 mills for sugar, oil, and flour; 8 distilleries, 2 'atafonas' for grinding mandioca, 2 saw-mills, 1 brewery, 4 tanyards, 1 tobacco-factory, 7 blacksmiths, 11 shoemakers, 6 tailors, 3 waggon-makers, 3 carpenters, 1 hatter, 1 stone-cutter, and 40 shopkeepers. There are 9 schools, Catholic and Protestant, most of the inhabitants being of the latter persuasion; of the total 259 families, there are 195 Protestant, 54 Catholic, and 10 mixed. The colony includes, besides the village of Paquara, six 'picadas' or farming districts, between Cima da Serra, Padre Eterno, and the rivers Sinos and Tocano. Although this colony has been such a brilliant success, it is said that the founder did not make a great fortune by it.

Conventos was founded in 1853 by Fialho

Pereyra & Co., and is now the property of Fialho and Vargas, who brought out a number of families from Germany, gave them liberal advances for food, implements, and other necessaries; the colony was located in the fertile valley of the Taquary, on the Arroyo Forqueta, an affluent of that river, about 90 miles north-west of San Leopoldo, and 40 from the town of Taquary. Messrs. Vargas are said to have lost money in the enterprise, but the colony is getting on well, comprising 83 families, chiefly dedicated to the cultivation of beans, maize, wheat, and flax, from which last they manufacture some good home-made fabrics. They also produce annually some pipes of wine for their own consumption; the exports consist of maize, potatoes, and beans. .

Silva was founded in 1854 between Conventos and the town of Taquary on an area of 30,000 acres belonging to a wealthy Brazilian; and two years later Mariante and Estrella, all in the same rich valley, within easy reach of the great watercourses which form such easy highways. All these colonists are thriving.

Maratà also dates from the same period (1856), and takes its name from the Arroyo on which it is situated, an affluent of the Rio Cahy. The lands in question were purchased by Andreas Kochenburger and Peter Schreiner (in 1855), who divided them into 120 farm-lots, which they disposed of to countrymen of theirs: the colony comprises 88 families in 3 picadas, or groups—St. Catherine, St. Andrew, and Good Hope, the total population being 560 souls. There are 42 Protestant, 37 Catholic, and 9 mixed, families; the school is attended by 70 children. The colony possesses 6 oil or flour mills, 3 distilleries, 1 brewery, 2 atafonas, 3 carpenters, 2 shoemakers, and 3 tailors, besides 2 large shops. Maratà is 30 miles north-west of San Leopoldo, not far from Port Guimaraens, to which the New Hamburg Railway will probably be prolonged.

Santo Angelo derives its origin from a decree of the Provincial Legislature, dated November 30, 1855, which also ordered the establishment of another colony at Nova Petropolis. The first batch of settlers, 119 in number, arrived from Germany in 1857, being joined by 7 Germans from San Leopoldo. The locality of Santo Angelo was admirably chosen, in productive soil, between the Rio Jacuhy and the slopes of Sierra Geral, 50 miles from the town of Caxoeira, and 200 from Port Alegre: the Jacuhy is navigable the whole way from the colony to Port Alegre, and the colonists have two roads, one to the town of Caxoeira, another to the Jacuhy ford, 25 miles distant. The colony is supposed to cover 20,000 acres (29,500,000 square brazas), but barely one-fifth is actually settled on, the rest still awaits colonists. Farm-lots of 120 acres may be purchased for 45*l.* sterling, and smaller lots of 80 acres (100,000 square brazas) at 30*l.* Since the commencement the colony has been under the immediate and personal direction of Baron von Kalden, who is highly spoken of. The present population is 825, of which number one-third are German-Brazilians, and the rest from the Fatherland, except 22 from the Netherlands and France. There are 304 men, 245 women, and 276 children; forming 194 families. More than two-thirds (568) are Protestants, to whom the Legislature gave the sum of 400*l.* to build a chapel; the Catholics also have one, and there is a school for the children of each persuasion. There are 6 mills, 6 shops, 2 tanyards, 5 shoemakers, 2 tailors, 2 blacksmiths, 19 carpenters, 4 cartwrights, 1 saddler, and 5 stone-cutters. The annual exports of maize, tobacco, beans, rice, sugar-cane, &c. exceed 1,700*l.* in value, and the imports 1,300*l.*, leaving a balance of 400*l.* in favour of the colony. The stock comprises 313 horses, 473 horned cattle, 3,811 pigs, 25 sheep, 8 goats, and 5,933 poultry. Several of the products were sent to the Paris Exhibition, and the tobacco obtained a premium, being considered quite equal to that of the Sta Cruz colony. The latest annual returns show 42 births, 7 marriages, and 12 deaths.

Novo Petropolis was founded on the part of the Provincial Government by Counsellor Ferraz, between the Rio Cahy and Sierra Geral as an entrepôt between Port Alegre and Cima da Serra; about 32 miles north of San Leopoldo. In 1858, the first batch of 80 settlers arrived from Germany, the terms offered being the same as in the Sta Cruz colony, viz., each family purchased a farm-lot of 80 acres for 30*l.*, payable in five yearly instalments, and the colonists to repay in like manner any advances made in their favour, besides the cost of transport from Rio Grande to the colony. The situation is well chosen, and there are three roads; to Picada Feliz, 12 miles, and Port Guimaraens, 30 miles, both on the Rio Cahy; and to San Leopoldo. The area is 140,000,000 brazas, or 100,000 acres, of which

THE GERMAN COLONIES: THEIR ORIGIN. 141

one-fifth is actually under tillage. At first, much confusion was caused by the appointment of an improper manager, named Vidal, who was at last removed in March 1860, after wasting much money: he was succeeded by Mr. Frederick William Barthelemay, who restored order, marked out the boundaries of the settlers, and devoted much labour to the making of roads. There are now 344 farms, distributed in 8 groups or picadas, as follow:—

| | |
|---|---|
| Olinda . . . . . . . . | 76 |
| Imperial . . . . . . . | 120 |
| Piraja . . . . . . . . | 55 |
| Riachuelo . . . . . . . | 8 |
| Barros Pimentel . . . . . . | 30 |
| Sebastopol . . . . . . . | 26 |
| Christino . . . . . . . | 17 |
| Nova Petropolis . . . . . . | 12 |

These numbers do not include a group of 75 Americans, to whom the Imperial Government has given a land-grant between Barros Pimentel and the Arroyo Sinimbri. Many Americans, however, as well as others sent to Santo Angelo, left the colony in disgust; but they were not suitable people, being for the most part unmarried, unaccustomed to country work, and displeased with everything. The Government gave them a subsidy of 25 cents a day for their support, but they refused even to help in clearing roads through the forest for the colony.

The Government tried to oblige the German colonists to pay for their lands in this way, by employing them in forest-clearings and deducting half their wages on account of the sums (in all about 9,000*l.*) they owed the State; but the colonists flatly refused, alleging that they were so poor as hardly to be able to support their families, much less work for half wages. Since then the State has spent a good deal of money on roads, the average cost for a clearance 20 feet wide being about 50*l.* sterling per mile. The first settlers received some annoyances from the Bugres Indians, and even so late as 1867 a band of thirty of these savages kept for some time prowling about the colony, at last making an assault on Michael Kerber's mill, where they were repulsed with such spirit that they retired without having done injury. Between the colony and Cima da Serra is a place known as Campo dos Bugres, where these Indians formerly lived. It is proposed to prolong the road from Cima da Serra to Nonohay, in the direction of Matto Grosso. The lands of Novo Petropolis are too elevated for cotton or tobacco, being nearly on a level with the Sierra Geral table-land; but all kinds of wheat, flax, colza, maize, beans, &c. do remarkably well, and the colonists obtained numerous prizes and 'honourable mentions' at the Paris Exhibition. They raise as much flax as to suffice for all the home-made linen necessary for their own uses. The lands between the rivers Jacuhy and Cadea are found peculiarly suited for cereals. The population of this colony is returned at 991 souls.

Cima da Serra, otherwise called San Luis, is another of the colonies founded by the legislature of the province: it is situated in thick woods, and distant nearly 300 miles from San Leopoldo.

San Lorenzo was started by Mr. Jacob Reingantz, near Pelotas, in 1858. The Government pays a premium of 2*l*. a-head on whatever immigrants he brings out, Mr. Reingantz paying their passage from Germany, giving them supplies for the first year, and selling them farm-lots payable in instalments. The colony has been very successful, and comprises 1,637 souls, in 340 families, who cultivate 372 farms and raise large quantities of grain and vegetables for the Pelotas and Rio Grande markets. The colonists are as 3 Protestants to 1 Catholic and have two schools: they have a little steamer to carry produce to Rio Grande, the colony being advantageously situated on the slope of Serra dos Taipes, on the banks of the navigable river Camequan. The State has founded a colony called San Feliciano on the same river; it is still in its infancy, and these two are the only colonies in the southern part of the Province.

Santa Maria da Soledada, like so many other enterprises of this kind, was ruinous to its founder, Count de Montravel, who obtained a concession from the Provincial Legislature in 1855, and, along with some capitalists of Port Alegre, marked out the new colonial settlement between the Rio Cahy and its tributary Ferromeco. The first settlers arrived from Europe in 1857, and in the beginning he would only have Catholics, which caused the colony to lose its German character, being largely mixed with Dutch, Swiss, &c. The Count also was too lavish in his expenditure, and when the colonists were heavily indebted to him he found himself ruined and gave up the enterprise, then taken in by the other shareholders with the assistance of the 1mperial Government. The colony now prospers, having raised last year 83,000 bushels of grain, 240 cwt. of tobacco, and a large quantity of yerba, sugar, flax, and cotton. There are 7 mills, 4 churches, and a state school. The farming stock comprises 7,300 head, besides 7,224 pigs and 22,000 poultry. The colonists are 1,571 in number (330 families), nearly two-thirds Catholics, and three-fourths of the whole number Germans, the rest from Switzerland or the Low Countries. The colony lies some 40 miles NW. of San Leopoldo, and 20 N. of Port Guimaraes, the proposed station of the prolonged New Hamburg Railway.

Monte Alverne was founded by the Rio Grande Government in 1859, on lands adjacent to Santa Cruz, close to the Arroyo Castelhano, an affluent of the Taquary. It was at first treated as a branch of the Santa Cruz colony, and the colonists for some years suffered great poverty. They have a public school, and are about equal in number, Catholics and Protestants.

San Francisco d'Assis and San Nicolao were founded by the Provincial Government in 1859; the first on the head-waters of the Ibicuy, the second near Encrucilhada, besides a third far in the interior on the banks of the Upper Uruguay; but none of these have made progress owing to the distance and impenetrable woods.

Teutonia was founded by a company of German merchants who bought some lands on the Taquary

L

and imported 40 families to settle on them. There are now 600 farm-lots occupied or marked out, and as the soil is good and the situation favourable, this colony promises to be a great success. It is 20 miles from the town of Taquary and 12 miles from the river, being close to the colony of Estrella already mentioned.

Sinimbu was founded by Messrs. Holzweissig of Port Alegre in the district of Maquinè, far northward, on the line of the proposed railway to Santa Catalina; but until some such means of communication be established the colony must suffer from its extreme isolation.

Caseros is a kind of military colony established by the Imperial Government, near Lagoa Vermelha, 120 miles N. of San Leopoldo. It counts 65 men, 48 women, and 76 children, who have a chapel, school, and 46 wooden houses. Their stock consists of 104 head, and their crop consists chiefly of maize, besides 175 bushels of wheat and beans, and 12 cwt. of tobacco.

The inspector of colonies gives a shocking description of the immigrants engaged in New York by Mr. Bocayaba, in 1867, and brought to Brazil at the expense of the Imperial Government. A contingent of 157 of them was sent to Port Alegre to be distributed among the new colonies in formation. A few that were married turned out well, but the rest are described as idle, worthless vagabonds, of whom only 13 were native Americans, and the others a mixture of English, Irish, Scotch, French, and Germans, that the police-authorities of New York (as the inspector insinuates) prevailed on Mr. Bocayaba to ship for Brazil with the hope of reforming them in the southern hemisphere. They arrived half-naked and shoeless, and insisted on the Government providing them with clothing: they refused to cook their own food and obliged the authorities to find them a cook; they bartered their bread for liquor, and to complete their misconduct burned all the benches, doors, and windows for fuel. On their way to the interior they committed some robberies and caused much trouble, and arriving at Nova Petropolis repeated their vandalism in the emigrants' house by burning all the wood-work and 100 yards of fencing. Some delay occurred in the payment of the subsidy promised them daily, and they proceeded to intimidate the authorities. Six of them were sent to Santo Angelo, where farm-lots and houses were given them, besides 2*l*. each in cash, but they took the earliest opportunity to run away, going probably to the Banda Oriental: 85

were sent to Novo Petropolis, most of whom also deserted. The inspector of colonies rejoices at this circumstance, for, he says, if they remained they would cause endless confusion. His report may be rather exaggerated, but it is impossible to shut our eyes to the fact that this kind of colonists was wholly unsuitable and the effort merely a waste of money.

Very different are the inspector's remarks on the German settlers, and I gladly add my testimony to the truth of what he says:—

'German immigration is the only kind that has done well in this province, and the success of these people is due to their patient and persevering industry in tilling the little farms they are proud to call their own, which they never could do in Germany. They are not only laborious, but also economical and able to bear privation or hardship, and hence their progress is sometimes slow, but always sure and steady. Look at what the first settlers had to go through in clearing the forests, facing the wild beasts and Indians, suffering want, exposure, and the effects of a new climate. But they overcame all obstacles, and in spite of ten years of war founded a vast and flourishing colonial system throughout our virgin forests. It is this plodding perseverance, patience under privation, and simple mode of life which make the Germans superior to any other kind of settlers in a new country.

'Meantime they have some defects, and the principal is a habit of routine which makes them averse to any change such as improved methods of agriculture or the use of machinery. In the United States, it is true, they imitate what they see around them and are carried along by the tide of improvement; but with us, who are rather sleepy in such matters, the German remains as conservative of old ways as if the world never advanced, and along with his simplicity of life and character (which is so admirable) he perpetuates the retrograde system of agriculture of past ages.

'The German settlers as a rule speak their own language exclusively, their children preserving this bond of nationality the same as if born in the Fatherland, but they also understand Portuguese perfectly. I do not share in the apprehensions of those who say it is injudicious to have so large and powerful a foreign element in the province. The settlers and their children have a warm regard for the country and speak of the Emperor with almost child-like affection. Neither are they of a troublesome or ambitious character, but entirely devoted to the care of their little families and farms, forgetful of returning to the Fatherland, and making themselves heart and soul identified with their adopted country, as happens in the United States and Australia, where they are esteemed among the best and most useful citizens.

'The Swiss are everyway as good as the Germans, possessing the same character and qualities, which fit them for colonists. The Portuguese have also many things to recommend them, being sober, steady, industrious people, fond of agriculture and the labour of vineyards. In Serra dos Quevedos, near Camaquan, there is a thriving Portuguese community, remarkable for its fine crops, its spinning and weaving industry, and orderly habits, which make it an example to our own native people of the surrounding country who are plunged in indolence and barely raise enough food to support life. And if we make an excursion to Faxinal de Cangussu, we find the grand-children of a lot of Portuguese settlers who came hither in the eighteenth century and perpetuated habits of order, virtue, and industry which are now well preserved by their descendants. When speaking of Portuguese I would also include people from the Spanish province of Galicia, who are very similar and equally laborious.'

For some years previous to 1860 the number of German arrivals averaged nearly two thousand, the Government paying a subsidy of 2*l*. per head to Messrs. Martin Valentin of Hamburg and Steinman & Co. of Antwerp on all such passengers. In 1860 this subsidy was suspended, and the immigration fell away more than half, at last dwindling down to 105 in 1866. During the Paraguayan war not much attention was given to colonisation, but at present a new era has begun which promises to increase largely the German and producing element of Rio Grande. The legislature has become convinced that whatever sums it expends in this way are speedily reimbursed by the enhanced revenue and productions of the colonists' industry. Several contracts have recently been signed for the introduction of German or Swiss settlers; one with Messrs. Holzweissig is for 40,000 immigrants. The Imperial Government has also contracted for 100,000 English colonists, at the rate of 10,000 yearly, to be sent out by a Bristol firm, and it is possible many of these will be settled in Rio Grande on account of its favourable climate and soil. Most of the Germans who come hither are from Pomerania or the Rhine-land, and one little district called Hundsweg, on the Rhine, has sent thousands. Last year it was stated to Government that there were two thousand families in Pomerania anxious to come out, if the Government would pay their passage. The colonists now coming out will receive farm-lots in the same way as those who came before: they will have to clear away the dense forests which are the only obstacle to the husbandman. The province is large enough for the aggregate population of half-a-dozen of the smaller kingdoms of Europe.

## XIV.

*ARRIAL AND PELOTAS.*

FROM San Leopoldo returning to Port Alegre I halted a few days at the latter place and obtained from the Government a pamphlet published on the province by an engineer named Camargo, with much statistical and general information. Being desirous of visiting Pelotas, I took passage in the 'Guayiba' to Rio Grande. The night was so rough on the lake that almost everyone on board was sea-sick.

After a day's rest at Rio Grande I started with Mr. Crawford and his brother-in-law in a whale-boat for Arrial, and in three hours we cast anchor in view of Mr. Crawford's farm. The only incident on the voyage was shooting some black swans, which line the coast in thousands opposite Ilha dos Marineiros; but we could not pick up those we killed, for the sea was running so high and a stiff breeze filling our sails, that the boat was almost unmanageable and at times threatening to capsize. Our sailors were two good-humoured Portuguese, who knew their business well. As the wind was favourable we scarcely altered our course the whole way, keeping almost equidistant between the low sandy range of the mainland and the verdant island of Mariners, on which some neat farm-houses are observable. The coast-line from Rio Grande to Arrial is a succession of sand-hills for 20 miles without a sign of animal or vegetable life, and so heavy for riding that the voyage by whale-boat is the usual way of travelling.

Abreast of where we have cast anchor is the fazenda of Senhor Brun, who is believed to be descended from some English settler, possibly named Brown: the farm-house is a snug one, and the owner is said to be a very worthy old gentleman. While the sailors are wading in the shoal water, about to transfer us to a smaller boat, a market waggon comes down on the beach and José (for it is Mr. Crawford's gardener) drives into the water and takes us aboard a long narrow vehicle, such as one sees in the German colonies. After reaching *terra firma*, we meet old Mr. Brun on horseback, a hale-looking man for eighty summers.

A charming green lane, reminding me of the quiet country scenery in England, with over-arching trees and one or two cottages on either side, conducts us to the manor-house of Arrial, which is built in the ordinary Brazilian style, a flight of steps leading up to a spacious apartment like a ball-room, from which bed-rooms open off to the right and left: the basement is used for cellars and the like. Mr. Crawford purchased this place a few years ago for the trifling sum of 500*l*.: there are 40 acres of ground, one half planted with fruit-trees, the garden last year producing 100,000 oranges. A magnificent pine-tree, in the centre of the grounds, is ascended by a ladder, and from the branches views may be obtained of the whole country, Rio Grande being clear to the eye. After dinner we stroll through the garden, where some English apple and Monte Videan pear-trees are found among the tropical fruits of Brazil. This place is about fifty years old, having been laid out by a wealthy merchant of Rio Grande for a brother who had lost his reason. The proposed railway from Rio Grande to Pelotas would pass by here, bringing Arrial within half-an-hour of the former city. A delightful suburb for summer or winter residence might be laid out in these lovely green fields and plantations. Meantime Mr. Crawford intends to procure from home a steam-yacht, which will run over to Rio Grande in an hour (15 miles), and thus permit him to reside at Arrial if so disposed.

The sun was setting as we stood on the high ground at the edge of the estate, overlooking the vast lake, with the jungle and thickets that intervene. This range of meadow-land would be well suited for any number of counting-houses, and Mr. Crawford entertains some hope of selling the ground to advantage as soon as the railway is carried out. At present he only comes to Arrial for a month in the summer, leaving it all the rest of the year to a Portuguese capataz named José, who had recently married a smart Irish girl, daughter of one of the Pelotas colonists, and Mrs. José keeps the house in apple-pie order: she was born at Pelotas, but speaks English as well as her husband does Portuguese.

The programme for the morrow was as follows: Mr. Crawford having to return to Rio Grande, his brother-in-law and I were to start at daybreak for Poro Novo and Pelotas, taking a native guide who would bring back our horses, as we should return by steamer to Rio Grande. Sullen peals of thunder ushered in the morning, and a black cloud to northward presaged a coming storm; but the horses were saddled and we resolved to run our chances, although Mr. Crawford advised us to put off the journey for a day.

An hour's riding over heavy sand was very tiresome, and the view flat and cheerless, a house or a few cattle being seen at long intervals. As the sun rose we descried ahead of us a wood, which our guide pointed to, saying 'There is Poro Novo.' When we reached the village it seemed to have no inhabitants: we rode down a long avenue of trees interspersed with ruined ranchos, from which not even a dog started out, and came up to the church in the plaza: the church was closed, but in front was a pulperia, where we obtained a glass of cashass and a box of sardines, by way of breakfast. The pulpero complained that the place was going to the dogs, and on my asking him what other inhabitants there were besides himself, he mentioned a shoemaker, or rather a man who used to follow that calling, but had now taken to drink, seeing the wretched state of things. During our stay of half-an-hour I did not see a living being about the plaza or church, but our guide told me of a terrible occurrence which happened here a few years ago. The cura, an Italian priest named

Jeronimo, was murdered on the steps of the church after saying the Rosary on Ash Wednesday evening: the criminal was suspected, but never punished. The church, although in decay, is a tolerable edifice of the last century, my guide's grandfather having been christened there: the cemetery is attached, contrary to custom in these countries, but there is little need to consult public health in the dismal group of ruins which bears the inappropriate name of Poro Novo.

The storm was visibly rising as we emerged from the thickets into the open country, and our guide despaired of our reaching Pelotas before it came on. Col. Carneiro, a hospitable Brazilian, lived a few miles to the west of our course, and I proposed we should make for the friendly shelter; but the guide said that in so doing we would expose ourselves to the chance of not reaching Pelotas for some days, as the arroyos intervening would become swollen and impassable. From a high slope we could discern the fringe of timber which marked the course of the Rio San Gonzalo, as the Pelotas river is called. Bleak, swampy country now followed, with ranchos few and far between, while the thunder rolled over our heads, and the rain, like a cloud of dust, came sweeping down from the hills behind Pelotas. It was dismal enough, and we arranged our ponchos to meet the impending storm. At intervals in these swamps we have to proceed in Indian file, closely following our guide's steps, who tells us of different persons lost here from mistaking the passes between the lagoons, the bottom of which is generally a thick dark mud. At one place our guide halts in doubt, but speedily adopts the device of the Gauchos, in all such cases, of driving some animal of those grazing near across the stream. We had some difficulty in prevailing on a calf to show us the ford, and indeed it was so bad that I was not surprised at the reluctance of our four-footed 'vaqueano.'

The San Gonzalo woods were about 3 miles ahead of us, when the rain came down in torrents. The ground was so bad and uneven that we had to proceed cautiously. Before a quarter of an hour our ponchos were wet through; mine was 'guanaco,' and incorrectly supposed water-proof. The rain was very tropical, our poor horses reeling and staggering under its fury, while the thunder broke in deafening peals, and the lightning was so brilliant and beautiful as to lose its terrors.

It cleared up for a while as we reached the woods, through which there are bridle-paths in many directions, and the trees are so thick that hardly a drop of rain had penetrated. For half-a-mile or more this sylvan scenery was uninterrupted, the paths so narrow that with difficulty could two horsemen pass each other. A large potrero or pasture ground intervened between the wood and the river, and we could see vessels going down with produce from Pelotas, the turrets of the church marking the position of that town some few miles higher up. To our annoyance we found a strong wire fence completely cutting us off from the river's side where the boats lay for ferrying passengers over. In one place the wires were partly broken, and after much trouble we got our horses through, regardless of what our guide said, that the owner had men posted to fire at trespassers. A dozen peons, mostly black slaves, were at work on a kind of causeway from the river-bank to a warehouse close by, and of them we enquired when we should be able to get a boat; but they were very insolent and only grinned at us, while the rain poured down again in a perfect deluge. The ground all about was a morass. We hailed boats going up and down, but they heeded us not. Just then a canoe from the opposite bank shot across the river, here some 200 yards wide;

it brought food for the peons. After much bargaining, the boatmen agreed to pull us up the river to Pelotas for 10 milreis (1*l*.). We had to lie in the bottom of the canoe the better to prevent its capsizing; and on reaching the middle of the stream we felt the full force of the current, but the boatmen pulled gallantly through and made for the opposite bank, saying they had to fetch something from their house. We found a pulperia or grogshop, where we were glad to get a glass of cashass, for our clothes were now saturated and sticking to us. From this point to the town was five miles, and I proposed to my companion that we should walk instead of boating it, but as he had a sore foot we had no alternative.

Our guide from Arrial had started on his return journey before we crossed the river: the poor fellow was as wet as we were and had eaten nothing that day, but it is incredible what long journeys a gaucho will make on an empty stomach.

As we proceeded to re-enter the canoe, one of the men refused to come, saying his comrade could manage the canoe without him. We then found it was the intention to take us up to Pelotas under sail. It was no use our urging the danger of such a voyage, for canoes are bad enough when propelled by paddles, but with a sail the risk is tenfold. The rain still poured down in torrents, and we trusted ourselves to the frail vessel with some such feeling as that even a dip in the river could not make us wetter. The boatman, who told us he was a Portuguese, sat in the stern steering with one hand and managing the sail with the other, while he took off our attention from any unpleasant reflections about the bottom of the river by pointing out on the bank the scene of a great battle, at Paso dos Negros, in the civil war of 1840, and some saladeros: the latter are larger and better constructed than in the River Plate, the city of Pelotas being the centre of this business in Rio Grande, and killing over half-a-million cows yearly.

At times the canoe heeled over alarmingly as some bend in the river caused our sail to fill rather suddenly. The current was running very strong down-stream, and I begged the boatman to keep close to the bank, as I was no swimmer. He said the river was not very deep as he was steering, and added that he could not swim a stroke himself. Just then came a puff of wind, snapping the sail out of his grasp, and as it flapped for a moment I remained watching events with a conviction that in two minutes some of us would be holding on to the bottom of the canoe. He tacked —she shook and gave a slight plunge forward, and away we went merrily and without further mishap till reaching a wooden mole at a muddy landing-place where we leaped on shore. The moral of this tedious journey is, avoid canoes in general, but never risk your life in one with a sail.

There was no coach to take us up to the town, and as we landed we saw a group of mulatto peons at a pulperia door laughing at us; they were half-drunk and bore the marks of their calling in the saladeros, so we thought it wiser not to address them, but to ask the owner of the grog-shop to take care of our saddles while we proceeded on foot up town. It was over a mile and in places we had to wade through the pools in the road, all the time keeping in view the turrets of the church. At last we came to a large plaza on the top of the hill, and soon found our way to the Hotel Europa, which is kept by a fat Portuguese with half-a-dozen lazy waiters. A few doors distant was a clothes-shop where we bought flannel underclothing, and, in fact, a complete outfit; but on taking the paper-money out of my pocket to pay for these articles, I found it was almost reduced to pulp from the wetting we had got. The first thing we did in the hotel was to get a bottle of cashass, and, before putting on dry clothes, take a regular bath of this spirit, rubbing it well into the joints to prevent rheumatism or other ill effects. It is indeed a sovereign specific in such cases, as we also experienced on this occasion, for in half an hour we were entirely cured of the awful drenching, and took no cold.

Pelotas is a town of about 12,000 inhabitants, with some regular streets, but for the most straggling and only half-built, although in almost every block you come on one or more costly houses representing an outlay of several thousand pounds sterling. The place has an air of opulence, active trade, and growing importance, which is fully justified by the knowledge that it is the chief centre of the produce or export trade in this part of Brazil. It is the newest town in the province of Rio Grande, having been founded in the present century. The inhabitants, mostly Brazilian, are thriving, hospitable, and industrious, with a good deal of the Yankee spirit of going a-head, besides being remarkably wide-awake in business matters.

Before we were an hour in the hotel we had three or four invitations, and, accepting the first, went to dine with the principal apothecary, a young Brazilian who studied in England and has his diploma of pharmacy from a London college hung over his fireplace. He speaks English perfectly, although now three years here, and tells us there is no Englishman in the town except Mr. Stewart, an artist, who is travelling all over the empire, pencil in hand, making short stays in each town. After dinner Mr. Stewart came in; a quiet gentlemanly youth, with the dreamy look of a poet or painter until he brightened up in conversation: he told us he had been over half Brazil on foot, with his knapsack and crayons, and had sketches enough to fill a large album; everywhere he met with the greatest hospitality and kindness, the planters being loth to let him go. This reminds me of a German friend of mine in Monte Video, who teld me he was two years travelling in the interior of Brazil without spending a dollar, the planters being only too glad to find a European to talk to about the exterior world, and in this way he went from one plantation or 'fazenda' to another, being supplied with horses and attendants wherever he went: he also told me of a friend of his who was eleven years travelling in the same manner, and added that such a life has many charms not only from the novelty and freedom it supposes, but from the magnificent scenery of the country and the kindness you experience from perfect strangers wherever you go. It is a kind of lotus-eating life peculiarly captivating for a young man unfettered by family ties; being, moreover, harmless and free from the temptations of drink and low company; above all, it is the life for an artist.

In the evening we went to take tea with Mr. Cordeiro, the United States Consul, a native of Pelotas, but educated and naturalised in the Great Republic. He told us that the flourishing appearance of the town and its inhabitants was fully borne out by fact, mentioning a score of people each worth from 100,000*l.* upwards. The house nearly in front of his own belonged to one of these saladero nabobs, who had expended over 40,000*l.* on it, the front being of white marble. Foreigners who come to Pelotas usually do well, and the town is so healthy and picturesque that it is surprising there are no English settlers. The

Italians, who flood the River Plate countries, are here not to be met with: I saw one, who was playing a hurdy-gurdy. There are some well-furnished shops, belonging generally to Portuguese or natives. The streets are paved and clean, and as soon as the gas and water-supply, already begun, are completed, the city will have a very respectable appearance. In one of the outskirts is an enormous hospital building, not yet finished, and apparently too large for the place. The great want hitherto felt has been pure water, the only supply being from the San Gonzalo river, a little above the saladeros, which still infected the water more or less. The aqueduct now in construction is some 12 miles long, being drawn from the hills, which form an amphitheatre on the west side; and Mr. Cordeiro advised us to drive thither next morning, as it commanded the best scenery in the neighbourhood. We accordingly made arrangements with a coachman who was to call for us an hour before day, so as to profit of the cool hours of morning.

The outskirts of Pelotas have some elegant residences commanding views of the San Gonzalo valley. Our road lay in the direction of the cemetery, and this is the one by which the trade with the Banda Oriental Republic is carried on, sending thither imported goods in return for horned cattle. Here I may observe that the saladero trade in these parts of Brazil is said to be brisker whenever a civil war is going on in the Oriental Republic, the armies on both sides devoting their energies to sweeping off the cattle, which they drive across the frontier and sell to the saladeristas of Pelotas or their agents at Yaguaron. We met numerous bullock-carts with hides and other produce. Passing the handsome villa of Saint Amanda, we saw the sun rising, its first beams tipping with gold the outlines of the Cerros before us. The road is of tosca, and a leagne from town we cross a rivulet called La Fragata, where there are tea-gardens, a favourite resort of the citizens on holidays.

About ten miles from town the road branches off in two directions, one towards Yaguaron, the other towards the Cerros, and at this point is a capital wayside inn kept by a French Basque (from Basses Pyrénées) and his wife, who have everything scrupulously clean, their son and daughter being the civilest of waiters, and the *cuisine* reflecting much credit on madame the old lady. At breakfast we met a German engineer, engaged in surveying and marking the route for the new aqueduct. Shortly after leaving the inn we found the sun beginning to be hot, and my compassion was excited by seeing some poor negroes carrying small baskets on their head and trudging the way to town. I learned that this was a penance given them by their masters for some misdemeanour, instead of flogging them; and as niggers don't mind the sun, the only hard part was the having to walk ten miles each way, to bring back say a pound of sugar or a newspaper. These slaves very often escape across the frontier to Banda Oriental, and return again in two years, after which period no master can claim them.

Cachoeira, or 'the waterfall,' is the name of a picturesque and secluded spot in the Cerros, famous for picnics, and close to the springs from which the new water-supply is being taken. Here we halted for a rest. There is an old mill in ruins, about which snakes are numerous, and the orange-trees have their bark everywhere cut with initials of sentimental idlers: parrots abound here. The stream which forms the waterfall is the S^{ta} Barbara; the water is pure and limpid. This locality forms a portion of what is known as the Mendoza chacra or farm. The concessionaire of the water-supply is Signor Duran, who estimates the outlay at 50,000*l.* sterling, the aqueduct being simply pipes laid down from this point to the town of Pelotas, the distance being variously stated at 12 to 14 miles. The same gentleman is concessionaire for the proposed railway from Rio Grande to Pelotas (35 miles), about which he intends shortly going to England.

Near the waterfall we came upon half-a-dozen men putting up sheds for the workmen who will be engaged in the aqueduct. The foreman told us they were much annoyed with snakes: he expects the water will reach Pelotas before twelve months.

Our coachman now took us by a road which goes along a high ridge of the Cerros, with a pleasant and extensive view on either side. Farm-houses, surrounded with orange-trees and herds of cattle grazing in the valleys, succeed each other for some miles, until we descend into a little wood through which flows the Arroyo de Micaela, with rocks rising up on either side among the foliage; and here we give our horses a rest. From the top of the next slope we see Pelotas, and far away to the left Monte Bonito, where the Irish colony was located, one or two families still re-

maining. Crossing another arroyo called the
'Sauce,' we strike upon the road by which we
went out this morning. A small market-cart,
driven by an old woman with a cloak over her
head, passes us, coming from town; the coachman pointing to it, says, 'That woman is a
countrywoman of yours.' It was Mrs. Carpenter,
one of the survivors of the colony, who was left
fifteen years ago a widow with several small
children in this strange land, and must have
perished of want but for her assiduous industry,
trust in Providence, and the kind assistance of
many native ladies. She is still poor, but has
raised up a respectable family. Yonder she goes
in her ass-cart with the proceeds of the butter
she has sold in town; she little heeds the tropical
heat of the day, but is thinking of her family and
humble cottage at Monte Bonito. For twenty
years she has led this life, with many a wish, perhaps, to see again the wild hills of Glengariff,
where she was born; but that is impossible.
Those of the Monte Bonito colonists who went
down to Buenos Ayres and tried sheep-farming
have been for the most part very fortunate, and
are now wealthy estancieros.

Passing the cemetery we alighted. Some of the

monuments were of Carrara marble with bas-reliefs and statuary, the cost of which must have ranged as high as 1,000*l.* sterling.

In the afternoon we went to see the church of Pelotas (there is only one); it was undergoing repairs and a re-gilding of the ceiling: it is a good-sized, well proportioned edifice. The stranger will find little of interest, in the absence of public buildings, unless he go to see a saladero at work, which to my mind is one of the most sickening sights imaginable. The cattle are killed, cut up, and the flesh and hides hung up to dry almost as quickly as I can write it; but the peons are smeared with blood, the ground is a red sea, the smell is also what you must expect in such gigantic shambles, the flies are in myriads; however, when one is accustomed they tell me it is an interesting and pleasant occupation, and all experience shows that saladeros are healthy places to live in.

Before leaving Pelotas, I may observe that Mr. Cordeiro's father has a concession for laying tramways through the town, which are much wanted. From this town the traveller may proceed by steamer either upwards to Yaguaron or downwards to Rio Grande.

## XV.

### *YAGUARON AND LAKE MIRI.*

THE voyage by steamer from Pelotas to Yaguaron, 148 miles, is devoid of interest, except when you enter on Lake Mirim; the steamers are small and uncomfortable, and the water is often so low that a delay of some days occurs in getting on and off the shoals. Yaguaron is a neat, well-built town of 3,000 inhabitants, situated on a hill-slope near the mouth of the river of the same name. The public buildings consist of a church, school, barrack and custom-house, and if you ascend the hill on which the new cemetery is placed, you will obtain a fine view of the Banda Oriental country beyond the river. On the opposite bank is the village of Artigas, belonging to the Oriental Republic, a ferry-boat crossing to and from Yaguaron every half-hour. During the Oribe wars, 1842 to 1851, these two towns were very flourishing and a great business was done over the frontier, especially in killing cattle and shipping the hides, the Blancos and Colorados (alternately) making it a practice in their wars to confiscate the cows and horses of their adversaries. Yaguaron declined during the Paraguayan war, a large number of the male inhabitants either being drafted or having gone away. Artigas is said to exist chiefly by smuggling; but the dealers suffer so much from the contending factions, that it is by no means a thriving place, and once or twice a year the floods of the Yaguaron river threaten the lower part of the town with destruction.

There are few Europeans in these remote places. An Irishman named Flanagan, who has changed his name to Fernandez, is a master bricklayer at Artigas, and an industrious American, who has lived here thirty years, has a neat residence in the suburbs; his wife is a native and he has a fine family of sons and daughters. At Yaguaron there is an English carpenter named Fulcher, who came here with his wife and daughter in 1868 from Port Natal: there is also an Irishwoman, married to a Frenchman who keeps an hotel. The principal trader is Senhor Paseyro, a native of Old Spain, who has a saladero, tannery, and other establishments, on both banks of the river, his chief house of business being along the Yaguaron custom-house, but his residence is in Artigas : he is very kind and attentive to strangers, and understands some English.

From Yaguaron the traveller may proceed inland on horseback to Bargé, Alegrete, &c., passing through a very diversified country and meeting with a welcome at whatever estancias he may pass *en route*: it is essential to have a good guide. If he wish to see something of Banda Oriental, he can take the weekly diligence from Artigas to Melo, a stretch of sixty miles of the wildest scenery, by Conventos, Corral de Piedra and other localities associated with terrible records of blood. Scarcely a dozen habitations are met on the way, and more timber than cattle, but little of either. It is not uncommon for the coaches to break down, and the conductor generally has a reserve of crowbars, &c., to splice an axle-tree or the like. The natives along the route have so bad a reputation that people dislike travelling singly on horseback. Before reaching Villa Melo, otherwise called Cerro Largo, there is a fine stone bridge built ten years ago by an enterprising Frenchman, who was murdered soon after by a native who objected to pay the toll. Melo is an interesting town, built by the Spaniards in the last century as a kind of head-quarters for this frontier. It has now about 4,000 inhabitants, several good shops, 4 closed banks, an excellent hotel, a prison generally full of bandits from the adjacent woods, a fine state-school, and some pretty gardens in the outskirts; an American named J. B. Lockett has a farm on a hill near the town. This place is 300 miles from Monte Video, through a wild and desolate country which is traversed by diligencia in three days, if the rivers be not swollen. The telegraph wires from Monte Video to Yaguaron will pass by here.

But the pleasantest trip from Yaguaron is to the Rincon de Ramirez on the banks of Lake Mini. The Indians used to call Lake Patos the Lagoa Guazir or big-lake, and Mirim (which is smaller) El Mini or the little; but the Portuguese adhere to the name of Mirim. It is 120 miles long and 16 wide, is fed by thirty-three rivers, its waters being for the most part very shallow: there are three great banks or shoals, Juncal, Zapata, and Sarandy. By the treaty of 1853 the lake is declared Brazilian territory; at present it is virtually closed to commerce on the side of the Oriental Republic, although now and then a boat laden with tiles or lumber, from Yaguaron or Pelotas, may be seen ascending the Sarandi or Taquary, which are navigable for miles.

Rincon de Ramirez is a kind of peninsula, with a coast-line of 20 miles on Lake Mini and having the river Taquary for its inland boundary: its area is 500,000 acres, and it takes its name from old Ramirez, a native of Andalusia and shopkeeper of M.Video, who bought this immense property for the sum of 5,000 silver dollars, and came to settle in this wilderness A.D. 1798. Until recently the mud rancho was standing in which he lived for many years, during which strange and varying fortunes visited this part of the country. The wars of Artigas devastated the Banda Oriental to such a degree that the Rincon de Ramirez was left bare of cattle except such *alzada* or wild animals as hid in the woods. Nevertheless so rapid was the subsequent multiplication of stock that in 1845 the Rincon counted 150,000 cows and 50,000 horses. The wars of Oribe then ensued, and at their close in 1851 the total stock did not amount to 20,000 head. At present there are 60,000 cows, 160,000 sheep, and 6,000 horses; the land value of the Rincon is about 200,000*l*. sterling. Two-thirds of the area have been broken up and sold to the joint-stock farming companies of Merinos, Mini, and

Cebollati, of which the shareholders are M. Videan capitalists and English residents. Sor. Ramirez, son of the original owner, still holds about 24 square leagues or 150,000 acres; his estancia house, La Feja, is on the banks of the Taquary; it is well-built and commodious, in the Brazilian style, and if you chance to find the proprietor at home, or any of his sons, you may count on a hospitable reception. A short mile distant is Sagrera's wayside inn and general camp-store, where the people of the Rincon procure clothing, groceries, &c., for which the old man makes a yearly trip to M.Video: during the wars of 1851 he was a captain, but now he leads a retired life here, with his sisters, one of whom has pleasant recollections of a visit to Cork and the banks of the Lee many years ago. Sagrera's daughter is wife of Sor. Breschi, manager of the Mini estancia, and speaks English perfectly, having been educated by Miss Edye at M. Video. From Sagrera's it is a picturesque ride to follow the course of the Taquary to the farm of Harismendy, an industrious Basque, who is on shares with Sor. Ramirez: his house overlooks the pass of the Taquary where the coach-road crosses towards Artigas and Yaguaron, eight leagues distant. Cattle for the saladeros of Pelotas are also driven across here: the river is about 60 yards wide, with steep banks covered with luxuriant timber, the stately palm giving its name to the neighbouring estancia of El Palmar.

The Rincon suffered not only from wars but from two successive plagues, first of tigers, secondly of wild dogs. About fifty years ago tigers were so numerous that Ramirez offered 3 dollars a head, besides allowing the hunter to keep the skin, which had a marketable value of six to seven dollars. In one year a fellow nicknamed Yuca-Tigre killed 105, and Juan Silva, between 1825 and 1830, received payment on 200 heads, or nearly half the entire number killed in that period. The wild-dogs were many years later, and Ramirez paid 2 reals (10 pence) a tail, till 20,000 were killed and the plague ceased: he states that in two years, from 1849 to 1851, he paid for 5,000 tails. These wild dogs used to cause much havoc among the calves, and on a few occasions were known to pursue a single rider just like a pack of wolves; if they overtook a man on foot he was a certain victim.

The estancia Palmar, about a league from Harismendy's, has a fine two-story house with a mirador or watch-tower, and stands on the spot where old Ramirez had his rancho in the days of contrabandists, Farapos, civil wars, &c., when he seldom slept in his rancho at night, but hid himself in the neighbouring thickets of the Taquary. A peach plantation surrounds the house, which is now the abode of a widowed sister of Sor. Ramirez: there is no idea of comfort within, but a cold, almost dismal, look, unless you ascend to the azotea, from which you have a beautiful panorama, the hills of Yaguaron being plainly visible beyond the Taquary. Pushing on towards the lake you pass the house of Louis Correa Pintado, whose daughters make excellent bread and keep a tidy home. After crossing some ugly streams you come in sight of Catumbera, the residence of a kind, hospitable Brazilian named Grimecindo Mattos, who is surrounded by troops of children and grandchildren. The house is built on what is known as a terre-moto or Indian burying-place (in the time of the Charruas), and here was found a box of bones, which, however, may have been the remains of some Spanish soldiers, who had numerous lookouts against smugglers. The traveller could spend some days very pleasantly with Sor. Mattos, and find plenty of game, from bandurria (a kind of water-fowl) to tigers and ostriches. He must beware of tying his horse under a tree called

Arueda, which has the effect of causing the body of man or horse to swell if they rest under it, although the native women have herbs for curing the same. It is not so easy to cure the bite of a Vivora de Cruz, a small snake or viper which is often met with and takes its name from a cross on its head. There is a bleak range of country with tufts of pampa grass ten feet high, from Catumbera to Charqueada on the bank of Lake Mini. Here are the ruins of a saladero built by Ramirez, where one or two Indians still remain: these men are splendid swimmers. The last European that lived here was an Englishman named E. B. Goss, from Liverpool, who was book-keeper, in 1862, when the saladero was working. The banks of the lake are a succession of low sand-hills, so white and fantastically shaped that at a distance they sometimes resemble houses, walls, flocks of sheep, &c. There is no sign of estancias or cattle to be seen for miles: the water is of a light green and so shallow that you may walk out 500 yards before you find it up to your knees. Yon promontory is known as Rabo Fiero, famous for tigers; and that island, called Isla de Hambre, derives its name from the fact that a band of smugglers who took refuge there died of hunger. Smuggling was not looked on as very dishonourable at that time, and it is said some of the first families in the River Plate have records of daring adventures by their ancestors in running the gauntlet of the Spanish guards.

If you are in quest of tigers you will be very likely to find some at the mouth of the Sarandi, where there are woods and cave jungles: they generally live by cattle-stealing, and will carry off a fat calf at night to their lair, but if they have once tasted human flesh they will eat nothing else afterwards if they can help it, and are known as 'tigre cebado,' so terrible to the natives that they then turn out in full force and never rest till they have killed him. A tiger that is not 'cebado' will hardly attack a man, unless in self-defence. On the banks of the Sarandi is a comfortable farm-house belonging to José Francisco Larrosa, who has a well-educated family and fine establishment; his pigs and Rambouillet sheep are famous in this part of the country, and his estancia, which he has on halves from Ramirez, comprises 11 leagues or 70,000 acres of good land: he grows sugar-cane to fatten the sheep. His next neighbour, ten miles distant, is an Irishman named John Roberts, from Cork, who has the management of several thousand sheep belonging to Los Merinos joint-stock

Company. The Sarandi at Larrosa's is 30 yards wide, and hard to cross after rain. Between here and the lake are some enormous ant-hills, three or four feet high. Arroyo Malo has plenty of water-fowl. Arroyo Lapota is infested with tigers, as you will learn if you halt at Major Muslera's house; his family also suffer from ghosts, owing to the usual cause, the house having been built on a terre-moto of the Charruas. El Mini is another of the joint-stock farming companies in which Messrs. Ramirez, Jackson, Fernandez, O'Neill, &c. have embarked, and here they have built a fine house on top of a hill which commands an extensive view. The estancia has an area of nearly 100,000 acres (14 leagues), comprising numerous rivers, fringed with timber, debouching into Lake Mini. The company was formed in 1868, with a capital of 55,000*l*. Mr. Breschi, the manager, and his wife, are very hospitable.

The estancia of Atalaya, where the present Mr. Ramirez resided for thirty years before building La Teja, is on a commanding hill at the entrance to the Rincon, and constructed as a fortress, to prevent freebooters carrying away cattle. The word Atalaya signifies a watch-tower. On one side is the river Taquary, on the other the Arroyo

Tapota, each about two miles distant, with a long fringe of timber which abounds in game. The whole territory of the Rincon is spread out at your feet. The house is a solid quadrangle of stone, with an inscription in dog Latin over the entrance to the effect that it was built by Gulielmus Fowler, A.D. 1839, and the exterior has only one window, which is strongly barred and formerly served as a shop, for Mr. Ramirez used to keep a general store to supply the wants of the neighbours, and as passers-by in those times were often unpleasant visitants, there was no shop-door, but the barred windows always allowed room for a bottle or a pair of boots to be passed through. The flat roof rendered the fortress complete, and the inmates could stand a siege of any odds or duration. But when you enter the court-yard you find Mr. Fowler's inscription was premature, for the house has not been finished, and the range of apartments on one side has never been roofed, while the doors and windows are wanting in another. Two sides of the quadrangle are inhabited by the manager, his family, and some Irish peons from South Africa. Ostriches are to be counted by the dozen hereabouts, but you must not shoot or 'bolear' them without special permission from the owner of the ground;

they are valuable not only for the feathers but also for the eggs, which make excellent omelets and often form a portion of the peons' food. Half an hour's ride from the Atalaya is a hill which has been dug up in all directions by disappointed treasure-seekers, an old native woman of reputed wealth having lived here, and no one ever knew what became of her money, if she had any. The ruins of her house are still standing.

From the Atalaya to Yaguaron is a ride of four hours, the distance to Artigas being ten leagues, and then across by the ferry. There are several streams and thickets on the way which were formerly infested by 'matreros,' and one place which now serves as a wayside inn and is kept by a German has the unenviable notoriety of two families who resided there having been murdered successively. The lawless condition of the Oriental Republic is indicated by the iron bars on all the windows, which you never see when you cross the frontier into Brazil. Even at present it would not be well for a single traveller to ride about the Rincon de Ramirez unless he had a trusty 'vaqueano' or guide, and a good revolver: the thickets or banks of rivers are often dangerous, and only three years ago there was in the prison of Cerro Largo a fellow named Fernandez who confessed to have murdered over twenty persons; he had not the least remorse for it, and was so fond of display that the fringe of his poncho was hung with silver two-real pieces. It is more than probable he is again at large, not 100 miles from these parts. The townsfolk of Cerro Largo, when the order came to remit him to M. Video, knowing that assassins invariably got free again in a few months, proposed to bribe the escort to shoot him on the way and allege that he had tried to escape; but a revolution broke out soon after, and the order for his removal was countermanded. It often happens in these revolutions that a 'guapo,' one who has murdered several people, is released from prison and promoted.

If time and companions offer, the traveller might make a pleasant journey from Yaguaron to the gold-washings of Cunapiru near Sant-Ana do Livramento, which are partly in Oriental, partly in Brazilian, territory. General Goyo Suarez, Mr. Rogers, and others have establishments there.

## XVI.

### GERMAN COLONIES IN SANTA CATHARINA AND OTHER PROVINCES.

BESIDES the colonies in Rio Grande there are others no less flourishing in Santa Catharina, San Paulo, Parana, Espirito Santo, Minas Geraes, and Rio Janeyro.

The Blumenau colony, in Santa Catharina, stands among the foremost for the numbers and wealth of its community, and takes its name from the founder, Dr. Hermann Blumenau, who afterwards transferred it to the State. The Paris Exhibition awarded it one of the special prizes set apart for institutions of most benefit to humanity; nor can anything be devised more beneficial for the surplus population of Europe than colonies such as this. Since its transfer to the Imperial Government this colony is known as Itajahy. Its first foundation dates August 4th, 1860; it has an area of 140,000 acres, of which about 4,000 are under crops. The population is 6,947, of whom two-thirds are Catholics, one-third Protestants, with chapels, schools, and cemeteries for each denomination. The annual returns show three times as many births as deaths. Besides such articles for their own consumption as sugar, rice, maize, wheat, and farinha, the colonists raise a large quantity of tobacco, their export returns showing 900*l*. worth of tobacco in rolls, and 4,800*l*. of sawn timber. Their imports amount to 8,500*l*. The colony counts no fewer than 73 saw-mills, distilleries, &c., and 6 schools. The farming stock is small, viz.— 306 horses, 987 cows, 26 goats, 1,431 pigs, 5,300 hens, and 205 bee-hives. The colonists have made 46 bridges, 48 miles of high roads, and 50 miles of bridle-path through the woods. Dr. Blumenau acts as agent at Hamburg for the Brazilian Government, and selects the most suitable emigrants, shipping them for even a lower rate of passage than they would have to pay to New York, the Imperial Treasury paying the difference. In 1868 he sent out 9 vessels with 1,097 adults and 489 children for this colony, charging the Government 26 thalers (say 4*l*.) per head for adults, and 20 for children; but in the following year he reduced it to 23 for adults and 17 for children. Thus the total cost of the emigrants to the Brazilian treasury, when landed in the country, is not much over 3l. per head, big and little. Two-thirds are Prussians, and the rest chiefly from Saxony, Hanover, &c., except 3 per cent. Austrians and Swedes.

Doña Francisca was founded by the State in 1847. The Hamburg Colonisation Company sends out 400 settlers yearly, at the same time constructing a road 160 miles in length, and purchasing from Government at a reasonable price 100,000 acres along the route of the same. The colonists are chiefly natives of Prussia, and nothing can be more flourishing than their condition: they have their own municipal council, and their exports annually rise to a high value. This colony is now more generally called San Francisco. The population numbers 5,237, including the village of Joinville, which counts 1,172 souls. They are nearly all Protestants, there being only 734 Catholics. There are pastors of both persuasions, and 12 schools, attended by 561 children. The Minister of Agriculture reports as usual that the colonists are industrious, and crime of any kind is unknown. They have 35 sugar-factories, and 77 mills and distilleries, of which three are driven by steam-power. Their exports consist of timber, cigars, arrow-root, butter, hides tanned, rice, sugar, &c. to the value of 21,000*l.*, their imports amounting to 18,000*l.* They have 2,465 cows and horses, besides swine and poultry in great numbers, and 413 bee-hives. There are 110 miles of roads in the colony, and the State spends about 1,200*l.* a year in making new ones. The great highroad to the Ignassia and Negro valleys in the province of Parana, of which 20 miles are made, has already cost 16,000*l.*

An English colony called Principe Don Pedro proved a failure. The ship 'Florence Shipman' brought out in 1868 some hundreds of Irish and English settlers from Wednesbury, who had little or no knowledge of farming. On their arrival at Rio Janeyro they were met by the Emperor in person, who conducted them to the nearest church to assist at a Mass of Thanksgiving, and then handed them over to his Ministers to be provided for. The lands unfortunately were ill-chosen, or at least the place where the colonists' huts were put up, for an inundation occurring some weeks after, it washed away the huts, drowned two of the settlers, and so discouraged the rest that the colony was broken up and the Brazilian Government very generously provided the poor people with passage back to England.

The province of San Paulo counted 40 colonies so far back as 1859, all of which were established by Brazilian planters, except Nova Germania founded by Karl Kruger. Some of them had only from 50 to 100 colonists, and the largest were:—

| | | | |
|---|---|---|---|
| Ibica, | founded by | Senator Vergueiro . . | 757 |
| San Geronimo, | ,, | Senator Gueiroz . . | 567 |
| San Lorenzo, | ,, | Luis de Songa Barros . | 444 |
| San Joaquin, | ,, | Dr. Lacerda . . . | 185 |
| Boa Vista, | ,, | Benedicto Camargo . . | 173 |
| Cauritinza, | ,, | Dr. Jordan . . . | 125 |
| Angelico, | ,, | Senator Vergueiro . . | 133 |
| Independencia, | ,, | Monteiro and Son . . | 121 |
| Saranjal, | ,, | Luciano Nogueira . . | 146 |
| Sete Quedas | ,, | Joaquin Amaral . . | 116 |
| Morro Azul, | ,, | Joaquin Camargo . . | 115 |
| Cresciumal | ,, | Senator Gueiroz . . | 100 |

Some of these afterwards burst up, the colonists alleging with much truth that they had been grossly deceived, and that their condition was little better than that of the slaves. As the Minister of Agriculture says in his report to the Legisture, it is culpable to bring out Europeans to work in Brazil unless on their own ground, and the sweat of their toil should never be turned to the advantage of speculators or traffickers in labour. He adds that the conduct of the San Paulo planters not only disgusted the Imperial Government, but damaged so much the name of Brazil abroad that emigration was greatly checked.

The only State colony now existing in San Paulo is Cananeo, which counts 623 settlers, mostly Swiss, who are indebted to Government more than 2,000*l.* for advances. Their annual produce, in maize, beans, rice, coffee, sugar, &c., is valued at 3,700*l.*, each settler having a farm-lot of 100 brazos square, say 13 acres English. In 1868 some Irishmen were sent here, but they did not like the idea of making roads in the colony, or cutting timber in D. Alfonso Bulhaw's saw-mill at Guaraha for wages much lower than some of their friends were earning on the San Paulo Railway. They made their way afoot to Santos, where the British Consul at once found them employment, except one Samuel Keats, a musical-instrument maker, who got back to Rio Janeyro and there procured an engagement at his trade. Some Englishmen and Germans were working at the Guaraha sawmill when the Government commissioner, Dr. Continho, arrived there, but the poor people's wages were so much in arrear that disorders were apprehended.

The San Paulo Government has just concluded a contract for the introduction of several thousand Germans within five years, and as the climate and soil are favourable, it is likely this Province will soon compete with Rio Grande and Santa Catharina in the way of colonisation. An English enterprise with a capital of 250,000*l*. has been recently started, the nature of which is thus set forth in the prospectus :

'The Company has purchased the " Angelica " Estate, situated in the Province of San Paulo, containing about 26,000 acres, of which a large portion is coffee land of the first quality. The buildings on the estate comprise a stone dwelling house, houses for colonists, substantial and large stores, and coffee and saw-mills driven by water power. The estate is under the management of Mr. Karl Koch, a German gentleman, who has had over fifteen years' experience in the management of coffee estates in Brazil.

'The existing coffee plantations on the estate comprise about 780 acres, having thereon 200,000 bearing trees (which yielded, in 1870, 27,239 alqueires = 5,600 cwt. of coffee), and 100,000 young trees. They are at this time chiefly cultivated by colonist families, who will form the nucleus for the extension of the colony under the Government Emigration Contract. The Company contemplates the employment of 1,200 families in the cultivation of about 8,000 acres to be planted with coffee. The yield from the estate will be annually increased as the existing young trees, and those to be planted, come into bearing, and may, when the whole of the plantations are in full bearing, be estimated to reach at least 90,000 cwt. of coffee.

The price to be paid for the estate and the Government contract is 126,000*l*. Of this amount the vendors (the New London and Brazilian Bank) take 50,000*l*. in fully paid-up shares of the Company, and guarantee upon the amount paid up on the share capital of the Company an average dividend of not less than 7 per cent. per annum during the first three years from the date of allotment.

'For the purpose of encouraging European emigration to Brazil, in view of the abolition of slave labour throughout the Empire, the Brazilian Government has granted to this Company important subsidies, estimated to produce 128,000*l*., in addition to an annual payment of 48,000 milreis during five years, which will at the exchange of 24*d*. amount to 24,000*l*. The Company will thus be enabled to offer to emigrants more than ordinary inducements and advantages, and it has reason to believe, on the authority of gentlemen of great experience in emigration matters, both here and in Hamburg, that a considerable number of emigrants will gladly avail themselves of the same.

'The "Angelica" Estate is eminently fitted for the reception of emigrants; it is watered by two rivers, has extensive woods, with timber suitable for all purposes, and is distant only 60 miles from Campinas, to which town the railway will be opened in the spring, and 10 miles from the thriving town of Rio Claro, which has a large German community.

'The Province of San Paulo contains an area of about 100,000 square miles, and is the most celebrated in Brazil for the good quality of its coffee and the large average yield per acre. Its climate is one of the most healthy in the world, and the largest portion of the Province being at an elevation of 2,500 feet above the sea, the heat is not excessive. As regards the progress of the Province and the fertility of its soil, no better evidence can be given than the figures contained in the latest published official returns, which show the value of the exports from the port of Santos to have risen from 131,443$l$. in the year 1848, to 1,974,919$l$. in the year 1871.

'As regards the communication between the Estate and the Port of Santos, the San Paulo Railway (the most successful railway in Brazil) runs in a direct line as far as Jundiahy—a distance of 87 miles; and the extension of this line to Campinas —another 17 miles —will be almost immediately opened for traffic. For the remaining distance of 50 miles to the town of Rio Claro, a provincial company has already applied for a concession.'

The Imperial Government has concluded a contract with an English firm to send out 100,000 English agricultural settlers in a period of ten years, and these will probably be located in colonial groups over the three Provinces of San Paulo, Santa Catharina, and Rio Grande. The Brazilian Consul at Antwerp has, moreover, instructions to give free passages to all farming emigrants properly recommended, and send them out by Messrs. Ryde's steamers of the Belgian and Brazilian Mail line.

The Province of Paranà has two state colonies, besides that of Superaguy, founded by Senor Gentil, with 496 settlers.

Assunguy, in the district of Coritiba, consists chiefly of French farmers from Oran, in Algiers, whose crops were destroyed by locusts in 1868. Having sent an envoy, M. Huet, to look out for suitable lands in Brazil, this gentleman went over the Provinces of San Paulo and Paraná, at last fixing on the department of Coritiba. The only lands that could be given gratis were covered with forest; and as M. Huet told the President that his countrymen were more accustomed to ploughing than felling timber, and had not money to buy cleared land, the Imperial Government came to their aid and advanced to Messrs. Huet, Imbert, and Schaeffer the sum of 431*l*., with which they bought a fine fazenda near Coritiba : the 'Polymnie' soon arrived from Marseilles with the first batch of ninety colonists, who were afterwards joined by others from that port and a small number of Germans.

Theresa was founded many years ago by the Imperial Government with 250 colonists, near Ponta Grossa at the confluence of the Ivahy and Paraná rivers. Its extreme remoteness has prevented its growth, and it is unadvisable to send Europeans so far into the interior; but the principal object was to establish a centre of population in so important a geographical locality, which was also on the direct route to the distant inland province of Matto Grosso. As soon as roads with the seaboard cities and provinces be established, this place must command an important future.

Besides the Germans there are 17 French, and the total population is 435: the land is mountainous, but they cultivate successfully sugar, tobacco, and cereals. They have a number of mills, distilleries, and kilns for making tiles. The colony is under the direction of Mr. Gustave Rumbelsperger, whose expenses of administration amount to 460*l*. per annum. The situation of this colony is marked on the map as 24·34 S. lat. and 53·45 W. long.

The Province of Espirito Santo has three state-colonies. Santa Isabel was founded some twenty years ago by the Imperial Government, and has now some thousands of flourishing settlers, who have been emancipated from all state-control and formed into a municipal community, after the manner of San Leopoldo and Itajahy.

Santa Leopoldina is of nearly the same date as the former, and has 2,000 inhabitants; but its progress has been retarded by the want of roads and the unfavourable nature of the ground. Messrs. Knorr & Co. of Hamburg annually send out fifty or a hundred settlers, at expense of Government, for this colony.

Rio Novo was founded several years ago by Major Dias da Silva, and subsequently purchased by the Imperial Government. As the colony suffered greatly for want of proper roads, the Government caused the Rio Novo to be cleared of obstacles and rendered navigable, since when it has progressed favourably. It is not exclusively European, but includes 328 natives, chiefly coloured people: the entire population is 734, forming 193 families, and cultivating 1,200 acres, under coffee, rice, beans, &c. The total area ceded to the colony is about 12,000 acres. Their annual crop averages 100 tons of coffee and 6,000 bushels of cereals. The colonists have petitioned Government for 500*l*. to put a bridge over the Rio Novo on the road to Itapemerim. A chapel is being built, and better schools are much needed, there being 200 children who can neither read nor write: of the adults 140 can read. The colonists are chiefly Catholics, there being only 59 Protestants.

The Province of Minas Geraes has two state-colonies. Pedro Segundo was founded some twenty years ago by the Union and Industria Company, which opened up the trade of this province by a magnificent highway of macadam, 91 miles long, to Petropolis, whence the Mauà Railway affords easy transit to Rio Janeyro. The colony is in the picturesque district of Juiz da Fora, and counts over 1,200 Germans, of whom two-thirds are Catholics. There is a resident German priest, and the Evangelical pastor of Petropolis attends to the Protestants, who number 379. The schools are attended by 141 children. The colonists have 3,000 acres under tillage, and derive great advantage from the good roads: they still owe the Union Company 6,700*l.* for advances or land sold to new settlers, of whom about fifty arrive yearly. By a contract with the Imperial Government the Union Company continue to manage the colony, besides a Modern Agricultural School, which is well worth visiting. The traveller who may happen to be at Rio Janeyro should make it a point to visit this colony, which is surrounded by magnificent scenery: he can proceed by the Pedro Segundo Railway to Entre Rios and Juiz da Fora, returning *viâ* Petropolis, the Mauà Railway and steamboat to Rio Janeyro. Numerous German settlers are also found about Petropolis; some of them are famous for the quaint and artistic walking-sticks which they carve out of the coffee-tree. One in particular, who lives on a hill overlooking the Emperor's palace, has beautiful *chefs-d'œuvre*, including cabinets, chimney-ornaments, &c. Petropolis enjoys a delightful climate even in the depth of summer, being at an elevation of 3,000 feet in the Sierra da Estrella, and is the residence of the Corps Diplomatique. Nothing can be more wonderful than the zigzag road, with stone battlements, which is cut as it were in galleries up the steep side of the mountain, connecting Petropolis with the Mauà Railway.

Mucury, in the district of Minas Novas, founded some twenty years ago by a Joint Stock Company, is now managed by a Government director, Dr. Carvalho Borges, and receives yearly 200 Saxons or other North Germans through Mr. Robert Schloback of Hamburg. The colony is situate on the confines of Minas Geraes and Bahia, comprising two groups, one at Ribeiras das Lages, the other at Philadelphia.

There are sundry other colonial settlements, some founded by Provincial Governments, some by private parties, and in many of which most or all of the colonists are natives. They may be briefly classified thus:—

*Province of Rio Janeyro.*

|   |   | Colonists. |
|---|---|---|
| Jacob Van Erven's . . counts | . | 2,354 |
| Wallao dos Veados . . . ,, | . | 540 |
| Independencia, of W. da Gama . ,, | . | 318 |
| Sta. Rosa, of Count Beaupendy . ,, | . | 142 |
| Sta. Justa, of Carneiro Bellens' . ,, | . | 123 |

*Maranhao.*

| | Colonists. |
|---|---|
| Arapapathy, founded by Government | 368 |
| Sta. Theresa, of M. Bittencourt | 140 |
| Pirucana, Joint-stock Company | 112 |

*Bahia.*

| | |
|---|---|
| Commandatuba, founded by Government | 290 |
| Engenho Novo, of Sor. Pereyra | 100 |

The Imperial Government has marked out 700,000,000 square brazos, or 835,000 acres, for new settlers: in farm-lots of 40 acres it would suffice for 21,000 families.

www.ingramcontent.com/pod-product-compliance
Lightning Source LLC
Chambersburg PA
CBHW020904230426
43666CB00008B/1307